IELTS Testbuilder 1
2nd Edition

SAM MCCARTER AND JUDITH ASH

macmillan
education

Macmillan Education
4 Crinan Street
London N1 9XW
A division of Macmillan Publishers Limited

Companies and representatives throughout the world

ISBN 978-0-230-47615-8

Original design by Peter Burgess
Page make-up by MPS Limited
Illustrated by ODI Ltd and Red Giraffe
Cover design by Jim Evoy

Authors' acknowledgements

The authors would like to thank the students of Reache Northwest.

The authors and publishers would like to thank the following for permission to reproduce their photographs:

Alamy/blickwinkel p117; **Getty Images**/PhotoDisc/ Robert Glusic p26; **PHOTODISC** p114; **Stockbyte**/PunchStock p55; **Thinkstock**/SarapulSar38 p87, **Thinkstock**/Szepy p50.

The authors and publishers are grateful for permission to reprint the following copyright material:

pp. 21–2 Extract from 'Play is the cornerstone of creative learning' by Kim Thomas © Kim Thomas, 2013. Originally published by The Guardian on 15 October 2013. Reprinted with permission. www.theguardian.com/uk; pp. 26–7 Extract from 'Why singing sand dunes hum certain notes' © Phys Org, 2012. Originally published by Phys.Org on 25 October 2012. www. phys .org; pp. 50–1 Extract from 'Are children consuming too much technology' by Matthew Yeomans © Matthew Yeomans, 2013. Originally published by The Guardian on 18 June 2013. Reprinted with permission. www.theguardian.com/uk; pp. 76–7 World Bank. 2010. *World Development Report 2010* © World Bank.http://siteresources.worldbank.org/INTWDR2010 /Resources/5287678-1226014527953/Chapter-1.pdf License: Creative Commons Attribution license (CC BY 3.0 IGO); pp. 87–8 Extract from 'Britain grows its own tea' by Jane Pettigrew © Tea and Coffee Trade Journal, 2006. Originally published by the Tea and Coffee Trade Journal on December 2006. www.teaandcoffee.net; pp. 108-9 Extract from 'History' and 'Licorice the Plant' © www.RealShopper.com Holdings Inc, 2014. Originally published by Licorice. org. www.licorice.org; pp. 117–8 Extract from 'Bird of Paradise: Dancer of the Jungle' © Papua Heritage Foundation, 2014. Reprinted with permission. www.Papuaerfgoed.org

Sample answer sheets and scoring bands (pp. 165–167) reproduced with permission of Cambridge English Language Assessment © UCLES 2015.

Printed and bound in Thailand

2019 2018 2017 2016 2015
10 9 8 7 6 5 4 3 2 1

Contents

Introduction

IELTS Testbuilder 1 prepares students for the Academic version of the International English Language Testing System (IELTS). It is more than just a book of practice tests. It not only enables students to practise doing tests like those in the examination itself, but it also provides invaluable further practice, guidance and explanation. This gives students thorough preparation for IELTS and increases their ability to perform well in the test.

This second edition of *IELTS Testbuilder 1* has been developed for students between score bands 5.5–7 who are working towards the Academic version of the IELTS test.

The second edition of *IELTS Testbuilder 1* contains:

Four complete practice tests for the Academic version of the International English Language Testing System

These tests closely reflect the level and types of questions to be found in the exam.

Further Practice and Guidance pages

In each practice test, Further Practice and Guidance pages follow each component or part of a component.

- For Reading and Listening, the Further Practice and Guidance pages contain exercises, questions, advice and tips directly related to each section or part of a section. They encourage students to reach their own decisions about what the answers in the tests should be. Their step-by-step approach enables students to develop and apply the correct processes when answering the questions in the exam.
- For Writing, there are language and development exercises and help with planning. There are also two possible answers at different levels for each Writing Task 1 and 2.
- For Speaking, there are examples of possible question areas, guidance in topic development and suggestions for useful language.

Key and explanation

This contains full explanations of answers to the questions in all four practice tests as well as answers to the exercises in the Further Practice and Guidance pages. For example, for multiple-choice and True/False/Not Given questions, there are clear and detailed explanations not only of the correct answer, but also of why other options are incorrect.

How to use *IELTS Testbuilder 1*

1   Students follow the instructions page by page. Students can complete one part of a paper, perhaps under exam conditions, and then either:
    - do the Further Practice and Guidance pages relating to that part. They can then review the answers given to the questions in the test in the light of what has been learnt from doing the Further Practice and Guidance pages. After that, they can check the answers to the questions in the test and go through the explanations.
    or
    - check the answers to the questions in the test and go through the explanations if there are no Further Practice and Guidance pages. They can then move on to the next part of the test.

    Note that in some cases students are advised to do the Further Practice and Guidance exercises *before* completing the relevant section of a component.

2   Students can also vary the order. They may wish to do some of the Further Practice and Guidance pages before answering the relevant questions in the test.

    As an alternative, teachers may wish to do the Further Practice and Guidance pages as discussion or pairwork, or ask students to prepare them before class.

The International English Language Testing System

The following is a brief summary of the four components of the Academic version of the IELTS test.

Listening approximately 30 minutes

Contents	Situations	Question type
There are four separate sections, which candidates hear only once. There are 40 questions. There is a short time (30–40 seconds) to read the questions before the recording is played and a brief time at the end of each section to check the answers. At the end, there are ten minutes to transfer the answers to the answer sheet. As the test progresses, the difficulty of the questions and tasks increases.	Sections 1 and 2 are usually of a general, social nature. In Section 1, there is a conversation between two people and in Section 2 there is usually a monologue, or an interview where one person does most of the speaking. In Sections 3 and 4, the contexts are of an educational or training nature. In Section 3, there is usually a conversation of up to four speakers and Section 4 usually contains a talk or a lecture of general academic interest.	The question types may include: • multiple-choice questions • sentence completion • short-answer questions • completion of charts/forms/notes/tables/summaries • flow chart completion • labelling a diagram/map/plan • matching • selection from a list

There is a range of native speaker accents (e.g. English, Scottish, Australian, New Zealand, American, Canadian, etc), as well as examples of some non-native speakers of English with clear accents. Speakers are of both genders, of different ages, and the speed of delivery in the recording is that of a native speaker of English.

Academic Reading 60 minutes

Contents	Texts	Question type
There are three reading passages with a total of approximately 2,700 words. Each reading passage has a minimum of approximately 750 words. There are 40 questions: usually two reading passages with 13 questions and one with 14 questions. Candidates must write their answers on the answer sheet as they answer the questions. There is no time at the end to transfer the answers. As the test progresses, the difficulty of the questions, tasks and reading passages increases.	The texts in the reading passages are on topics of a general nature, which are taken from books, journals, magazines and newspapers. The topics are not specific to any one discipline. They are all accessible to candidates who are entering undergraduate or postgraduate courses. There is at least one article which contains a detailed logical argument.	The question types may include: • multiple-choice questions • selection from a list • sentence completion • short-answer questions • completion of tables/charts/summaries/notes • flow chart completion • matching headings • matching information • matching sentence endings • identification of information (True/False/Not Given) • identification of a writer's views/claims (Yes/No/Not Given) • classification/matching features

Academic Writing 60 minutes

Contents	Task type	Assessment criteria
Writing Task 1 Candidates are advised to spend about 20 minutes on this task and write a minimum of 150 words.	Writing Task 1 usually includes a description of: data such as a graph, table, bar chart or pie chart; a process; a map or plan; or a diagram of how something works. There may be two or more sets of data to describe, e.g. a pie chart and a table.	In Writing Task 1, assessment is based on candidates' ability to summarize, organize and compare data where possible, describe the stages of a process, describe an object or event or explain how something works. Candidates' ability to use a range of vocabulary and grammatical structures, and their ability to complete the task are assessed.
Writing Task 2 Candidates are advised to spend about 40 minutes on this task and write a minimum of 250 words.	In Writing Task 2, candidates are given a point of view, argument or problem to write about.	In Writing Task 2, assessment is based on candidates' ability to write a solution to a problem; present and support an opinion; compare and contrast evidence and opinions; evaluate and challenge ideas, evidence or arguments.

Please note:
- in Writing Tasks 1 and 2, candidates are assessed on their ability to write in a style that is suitable for the task.
- Writing Task 2 contributes twice as much to the Writing score as Task 1.

Speaking 11–14 minutes

Contents	Task type	Assessment criteria
Part 1 Introduction and interview (4–5 minutes)	The examiner will introduce himself/herself, check the candidate's identification and then ask him/her questions about himself/herself, their home, interests and a wide range of familiar topics.	Candidates' ability to communicate effectively in English is assessed. This assessment includes: • Fluency and coherence: how well candidates speak without hesitating and the organization of their answers.
Part 2 Task card (3–4 minutes)	Candidates are given a task card with prompts and asked to talk on a particular topic. They are given one minute to prepare and can make notes to glance at as they speak. Pencil and paper are provided to make notes.	• Lexical resource: the candidates' range of vocabulary. • Grammatical range and accuracy: the range of grammar uses, for example the range of structures and complex sentences using connecting words: *because, for instance, and so, but* and so on.
Part 3 Two-way discussion (4–5 minutes)	Candidates take part in a discussion with the examiner where they are asked a series of questions. The questions are connected with Part 2, but they are of an abstract nature. Candidates need to give more detailed answers by explaining, evaluating and analysing.	• Pronunciation: how clear and intelligible candidates are when they speak.

For notes on how IELTS is scored, see page 167.

For further information about the exam, see also the IELTS Handbook and www.ielts.org. The website contains information about the public marking scores for the Writing and Speaking components.

Test 1

Listening approximately 30 minutes

Before you listen to the recording, read the test questions and go to the Further Practice and Guidance section on pages 14–15.

SECTION 1 *Questions 1–10* 🎧 1.1–1.6

Questions 1–3

Choose the correct letter, A, B or C.

> *Example*
>
> Maxine Johnson is a
> (A) garden designer.
> B   local builder.
> C   plumber.

1   Mr Bird has

     A   recently moved to the house.
     B   lived in the house for ages.
     C   just painted the house.

2   In the garden, Mr Bird has removed

     A   trees and cut the grass.
     B   rocks and cut down trees.
     C   rubbish and cut the grass.

3   How long is the garden?

     A   15 metres
     B   20 metres
     C   25 metres

Questions 4–6

Complete the table below.

Write NO MORE THAN THREE WORDS AND/OR A NUMBER for each answer.

Garden information		
Garden features	**Information**	**Size**
Patio	Wooden with table and chairs	**4** ....
Pond	Small and no **5** .... Fountain with lights	Approximately two metres across
Fence	With flowers and door into a **6** .... garden	Two metres high

Questions 7–10

Complete the form below.

*Write **NO MORE THAN _TWO WORDS_ AND/OR A _NUMBER_** for each answer.*

Contact details

Name:	*Mr Bird*
Email address:	7 ....
Possible to start on:	8 ....
Length of job:	9 ....
Work mobile:	10 ....

Stop the recording when you hear 'That is the end of Section 1.'

Now check your answers to Section 1 of the test.

SECTION 2 *Questions 11–20* 🎧 1.7–1.11

Questions 11–14

Complete the sentences below.

*Write **NO MORE THAN TWO WORDS** for each answer.*

City centre information

11 Martina predicts that there will be lots of people using the ....

12 Argent Street will be pedestrian-only on ....

13 The guides in the city centre wearing .... will help visitors with travel information.

14 The profits from the day's events will be given to ....

Questions 15–18

Label the map below.

*Write the correct letter, **A–I**, next to questions 15–18.*

Food of Life Festival

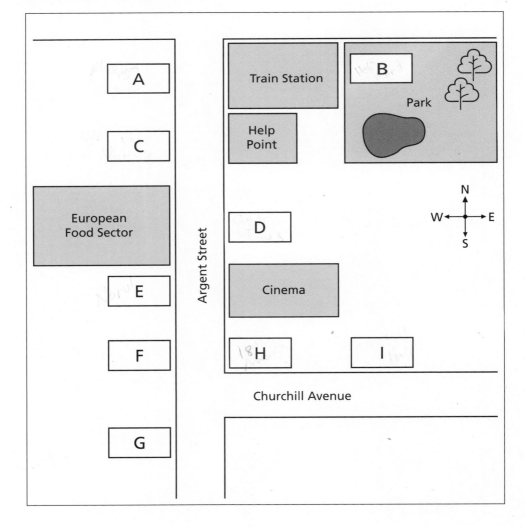

15   Asian sector   ....

16   Chocolate display   ....

17   Latin American display   ....

18   Cannery Hall   ....

Questions 19 and 20

*Choose **TWO** letters, A–E.*

Which **TWO** further attractions does the speaker mention?

A   a firework display

B   free food for adults

C   a film festival

D   shop discounts

E   music lessons

Stop the recording when you hear 'That is the end of Section 2.'

Now check your answers to Section 2 of the test.

SECTION 3   *Questions 21–30*   🎧 1.12–1.16

Questions 21–23

Choose the correct letter, A, B or C.

Antonia's writing

21   Antonia's essay is

    A   around 2,000 words over the limit.
    B   around 7,000 words over the limit.
    C   exactly 7,000 words in total.

22   To help her write, Antonia used the checklist

    A   given on the department website.
    B   put together by her and Cheng.
    C   handed out by her tutor, Dr Nakamura.

23   Antonia needs to check her work for

    A   mistakes and organization.
    B   references and mistakes.
    C   organization and references.

Questions 24–28

Complete the table below.

*Write **ONE WORD ONLY** for each answer.*

Solutions for Cheng's writing problems

Issue/Problem	Cause	Solution
Lack of 24 .... Difficulty focusing	No specific title Not sure what to focus on	Limit essay to: • one or two perspectives or • 25 .... in particular time: pre-Digital Age
Writing introduction	Ignorance of 26 .... involved in introductions	See Student Support pages on university website
27	Fear of returning to beginning again	Possibly, write a 28 .... of the essay

Questions 29 and 30

Complete the notes below.

*Write **NO MORE THAN TWO WORDS AND/OR A NUMBER** for each answer.*

Purpose of long essay: to encourage 29 ....

Essay to be submitted by: 30 ....

Stop the recording when you hear 'That is the end of Section 3.'

Now check your answers to Section 3 of the test.

SECTION 4   *Questions 31–40* 🎧 1.17–1.19

Complete the notes below.

Write **NO MORE THAN TWO WORDS AND/OR A NUMBER** *for each answer.*

Agriculture – re-greening the deserts of the world

Recorded talk available on website within 48 hours

Historical perspective

Between 8,000 and **31** .... years ago, Sahara: green and fertile

World temperature similar to present – weather not as **32** .... as before

African, Asian and American deserts: plenty of **33** .... in the past

Lake Chad equal in area to: France, Germany, Spain and **34** .... combined

In Algeria and southern Libya:

- discoveries of underground rivers
- bones of wild animals
- and **35** .... for producing grain

Modern day

Weather changes: complex and controversial

- not just about flooding, severe winter weather, storms, droughts, etc
- about impact on people's **36** ....

Europe

Warming up: wheat, barley and **37** .... not suitable for cultivation

Olives and grapes: more common in UK

Southern European countries: production of **38** .... severely limited

Consequences of weather changes

- higher **39** .... in Europe
- more **40** .... in desert regions, e.g. the Sahel
- increased chance of water in desert areas

Stop the recording when you hear 'That is the end of Section 4.'

Now check your answers to Section 4 of the test.

General Tips for the Listening component

- Listen to the instructions for each set of questions and use the time to skim the questions.
- Read the rubrics carefully and check word limits, etc.
- Process the questions as quickly as possible as you usually have only 30–40 seconds to do so. The time depends on the number and complexity of the questions.
- Use the headings and the instructions in the recording in each section to give you the context of the recording.
- Constantly predict what is coming next in terms of context and the answers as you listen. Use the questions and headings to help you.
- Remember the recording is played only once, so it is crucial that you concentrate throughout. It is important to learn to read, listen and write simultaneously.
- Write your answers in the test booklet. You have ten minutes at the end to transfer your answers to the answer sheet.
- Take care when transferring your answers. Make sure you put the answers in the correct box and make sure the spelling is correct.
- Make sure you are aware of the word limits in questions. Do not write words from the test itself on the answer sheet. You will be penalized for doing so.
- Check your answers after you transfer them.

Section 1: Prediction skills

Preparation for listening is an important part of the IELTS Listening component. Looking carefully at the questions can help you predict a number of things about what you are going to hear and the type of answer that is required. The following exercises help you to practise predicting skills.

Questions 1–3: Multiple-choice questions

In multiple-choice questions, read the stem and the options and try to build a picture using the information given.

Look at the stems and options in Questions 1–3 and the example on page 7. Decide which information below is true (*T*) or false (*F*).

1 Mr Bird lives in a house, not in a flat.   ....

2 Mr Bird has tidied up the garden.   ....

3 Mr Bird did two things to tidy up the garden.   ....

4 Mr Bird did three things to tidy up the garden.   ....

5 The garden is long.   ....

6 Mr Bird has asked a garden designer to help design the garden.   ....

Questions 4–10: Completing a table/notes (1)

It is important that you develop the skill of predicting the content of gaps in tables, sentences and notes.

1 Look at the rubric for Questions 4–6 on page 7 and decide what is required in each gap: a word, a number or both. Use the information in the table to help you: the details in each column give you the key words before the answer. Write questions:

Example:

Question 4: Is it a number? Is it a number and (a) word(s)? Is it a long number? What kind of word(s): an adjective, a noun, a noun phrase, a verb, an adverb?

2 Now write questions for gaps 5 and 6 in the table and Questions 7–10 in the form. Then predict what is required for each gap.

Section 2: Key words

It is also important to listen for key words in sentence completion tasks, in the stem and options of multiple-choice questions, in labels on maps and in selections from lists.

Remember you will often (but not always) hear synonyms or paraphrases of key words or phrases/sentences in the Listening test. The answer usually comes after the key words.

Look at Questions 11–14 on page 9. Underline key words or phrases to listen for and think of possible synonyms or paraphrases.

Section 4: Completing a table/notes (2)

In some questions, you are asked to answer short questions, complete sentences, complete tables or complete notes. In these types of tasks, think about:

- the word limit.
- the grammar of the sentences/notes.
- the grammar of the missing word(s) (adjective, noun, noun phrase, verb, adverb, number).

Try to predict possible answers.

Look at Questions 31–40 on page 13 and write down the key words that warn you the answer is about to be given. Then circle the grammar of the answer needed in each case.

31 Key word(s) ....
   Grammar   adjective | noun | noun phrase | verb | adverb | number

32 Key word(s) ....
   Grammar   adjective | noun | noun phrase | verb | adverb | number

33 Key word(s) ....
   Grammar   adjective | noun | noun phrase | verb | adverb | number

34 Key word(s) ....
   Grammar   adjective | noun | noun phrase | verb | adverb | number

35 Key word(s) ....
   Grammar   adjective | noun | noun phrase | verb | adverb | number

36 Key word(s) ....
   Grammar   adjective | noun | noun phrase | verb | adverb | number

37 Key word(s) ....
   Grammar   adjective | noun | noun phrase | verb | adverb | number

38 Key word(s) ....
   Grammar   adjective | noun | noun phrase | verb | adverb | number

39 Key word(s) ....
   Grammar   adjective | noun | noun phrase | verb | adverb | number

40 Key word(s) ....
   Grammar   adjective | noun | noun phrase | verb | adverb | number

The majority of the answers are ....

Why is this? ....

Now check your answers to these tasks. When you have done so, listen to the recording and complete Sections 1–4 on pages 7–13.

Academic Reading 60 minutes

READING PASSAGE 1

*You should spend about 20 minutes on **Questions 1–13**, which are based on Reading Passage 1 below.*

The Story of Platinum

The white metal platinum is much denser and rarer than gold, in fact some 30 times rarer. To acquire an ounce of platinum, it takes about ten tonnes of ore. Similar to gold, it is supposed to have come to the Earth in meteorites, the earliest recorded having hit the planet off the coast of western Greenland about three billion years ago.

The earliest recorded evidence of platinum use is in gold jewellery from Nubia with traces of platinum in 1200 BC and famously on a box from an Egyptian tomb in Thebes dating from 700 BC. Platinum also made appearances in pre-Columbian artefacts in South America, where platinum was used for decorative purposes to adorn the body including earrings and masks with the earliest known piece being that of a small platinum head. Evidence of platinum use did not appear again in South America until the time of the Incas, the most famous of the civilizations of South America. It was not until the time of the Spanish Conquistadors' arrival in South America in the 15th and 16th centuries that the first Europeans came into contact with platinum. It was, however, considered by the new arrivals as an inferior form of silver, from which it took its name *platina,* meaning small silver in Spanish. Ignorant of the skills of the local people, they were unable to melt it, so platinum was thrown back into rivers.

When platinum was finally identified and classified as a new metal in the 18th century it began to attract the interest of scientists in Europe. Being very hard and having a high melting point, however, it took time for scientists to develop ways to melt the metal. A concave mirror device created in 1758 by Macquer, a French scientist, managed to melt platinum, but the method was cumbersome. In 1786, a French court jeweller, Janety, used arsenic to create an alloy of platinum that was then refined to make pure platinum. In Spain and England, other experiments were carried out, but in 1782 Antoine Lavoisier succeeded in melting platinum using a high-temperature torch made from oxygen and hydrogen. Once melting was made possible, its use in making jewellery was greatly enhanced.

Platinum, as the other precious metals gold and silver before it, became a store of value. In jewellery, platinum accounts for only 30% of the approximate eight tonnes of the metal mined each year. Unlike gold, platinum does not wear away; in fact, because of its durability, the International Prototype Kilogram – stored at Sèvres in France – is made of platinum. Apart from its intrinsic value as a rare metal, platinum is desirable in jewellery for various reasons. Due to its very hardness, it is hypoallergenic, i.e. it does not cause allergy, unlike other metals such as gold; it does not reflect colour onto diamonds, which it can secure tightly as a result of strength and hardness.

Platinum is well known for its industrial use. The bulk of platinum is used in the car industry in areas such as catalytic converters as the platinum is able to absorb huge amounts of hydrogen, which makes it useful in environmental clean-up. The current manufacture of glass, as in the past, along with anti-cancer medication, fibre-optic cables and LCD displays are all reliant on platinum. It is also a key component of fuel cells, where it is used to convert hydrogen and oxygen into energy with water being the waste product.

Being a rare metal, platinum is only found in a few locations around the world. Up until the early part of the 19th century Colombia was the only source of platinum. Then in 1820, various deposits were discovered in the Ural Mountains in Russia, still a major source today. There are minor deposits in Montana in the USA, but the main supplier of platinum today is South Africa where the world's largest deposits were discovered in the mid-1920s.

Russia minted 1.5 million platinum coins, but ceased doing so when the value of the metal exceeded that of the coins. Today, various platinum coins, such as the Australian Koala and the Canadian Maple Leaf in 1988, the Chinese Panda in 1987, and the American Eagle in 1997, have been made available in one ounce sizes or less, and bars of platinum weighing ten ounces and smaller sizes for investment.

Questions 1–7

Do the following statements agree with the information given in Reading Passage 1?

Write

TRUE   *if the statement agrees with the information*

FALSE   *if the statement contradicts the information*

NOT GIVEN   *if there is no information on this*

1 Platinum is the least common metal on the planet.

2 The first known meteorite hit the Earth about three billion years ago.

3 The Incas are more well known than other past civilizations in South America.

4 Knowledge about platinum was widespread in Europe before the 15th century.

5 Like the Spanish Conquistadors, the scientists in Europe took little notice of platinum.

6 The main reason platinum was employed in making jewellery was because it was hard-wearing.

7 Platinum is no longer employed in the manufacture of glass.

Questions 8–10

Complete the sentences below.

*Choose **NO MORE THAN THREE WORDS** from the passage for each answer.*

8 Macquer's attempt at melting platinum was ....

9 Platinum was not common in jewellers' work until the development of a

high-temperature ....

10 As with gold and silver, platinum became a ....

Questions 11–13

*Choose **THREE** letters, A–F.*

The list below includes facts about platinum in the 20th century.

Which **THREE** are mentioned by the writer of the text?

A Platinum is mined in two main regions, Africa and Russia.

B South African platinum production began in the 19th century.

C Before 1820, the production of platinum was not common.

D Production of platinum is increasing in Russia.

E The American Eagle was introduced before the Australian and Canadian coins.

F The use of platinum is widespread in industry.

Before you check your answers to Reading Passage 1, go to pages 19–20.

General Tips for the Reading component

- Survey the whole test looking at the titles of the reading passages, the passages themselves and the questions. This should take about 20 seconds.
- Skim the title, the reading passage and the questions. Limit this stage of the reading process to two minutes. At this stage, it is important not to read in depth.
- Read the rubrics carefully and check: word limits; whether you can use answers more than once; and indications regarding the location of information.
- Read the questions and look for words and phrases that will help you locate the information in the passage.
- Find the information in the passage and read closely the part of the text that relates to the question.
- Be conscious of the time throughout. You have roughly 20 minutes for each reading passage and the questions. Note one of the passages will usually have 14 questions.
- Learn to leave questions that you find difficult and come back to them. Do not waste time.
- Write your answers directly onto the answer sheet as there is no time at the end to transfer answers.
- Make sure you write the answers in the correct boxes on the answer sheet.
- Make sure the spelling is correct.
- Make sure you are aware of the word limits in questions. Do not write words from the test itself on the answer sheet. You will be penalized.
- Review the answers on the answer sheet briefly before you move on to the next reading passage.

Tips

Questions 1–7: True/False/Not Given

- Read the rubric and note that this type of statement tests analysis of information in the passage.
- Skim all of the statements.
- Underline words that will help you locate the information in the reading passage.
- Underline or box grammar patterns in the statements, e.g. comparisons, purpose, reasons.
- Underline or box words related to quantity, frequency and positive and negative verbs and adjectives of evaluation. Use these patterns and words to help you analyse the text.
- Take care with comparison: two concepts or items may be mentioned in the text, but there may be no comparison. The same principle applies to 'cause and effect' and 'links'.
- Note that it is possible to have *Not Given* as the first answer and also to have only *True* and *False* answers, without *Not Given*, etc.

The questions below and on page 20 will help you to make sure you have chosen the correct answers for Questions 1–7 in Reading Passage 1.

Question 1 *Look at the first sentence of paragraph 1 and answer the questions below.*

1 Does the sentence mention that platinum is a metal? Is this a characteristic of platinum?
2 Does the sentence mention how rare platinum is?
3 Does the sentence compare the rareness of platinum with any other metal? Which one?
4 Are any other rare metals mentioned?
5 Bearing questions 1–4 in mind, is there enough information to tell you that platinum is the rarest metal on the planet?

Question 2 *Look at the third sentence of paragraph 1 and answer the questions below.*

1 Is information about a time mentioned? If so, what is it?
2 Does the time relate to *the earliest recorded meteorite*?
3 What does *the earliest recorded meteorite* mean? Does the *earliest recorded meteorite* mean the same as the first known meteorite?

Question 3 *Look at the third sentence of paragraph 2 and answer the questions below.*

1 Are the Incas mentioned in the third sentence?
2 Does the sentence mention that the Incas were the most famous South American civilization?
3 If so, does that mean that there is a comparison between the Incas and the other civilizations?

Question 4 *Look at the fourth sentence of paragraph 2 and answer the questions below.*

1 Does the sentence contain a reference to time? If so, what is it?
2 Which of these paraphrases does **not** paraphrase the text:

   a Not until [the time of the Spanish Conquistadors' arrival in South America in the 15th and 16th centuries] did [the first Europeans come into contact with platinum].
   b Before [...], Europeans had come into contact with ...
   c Only after [...] did Europeans come into contact with ...
   d Up to [...] Europeans had not come into contact with ...

3 Does the statement in Question 4 contain a time phrase? If so, what is it?
4 Is the time phrase in Question 4 mentioned in **2 a–d** above? If so, in which one?
5 Can you think of other ways of paraphrasing the time phrase 'before the 15th century' in the statement?

Question 5 *Look at the first sentence of paragraph 3 and answer the questions below.*

1 A good strategy to help you answer True/False/Not Given statements is to turn them into questions. Which word in statement 5 is stressed the most when you turn it into a question: *Spanish, Conquistadors, Europe* or *little*?
2 Does that mean you need to look for a paraphrase or the opposite of this word? Or both?
3 Is the word *little* negative or positive?
4 Which phrase contrasts with *take little notice of*?

Questions 6 and 7

Which words do you stress more when you change statements 6 and 7 into questions?

Now check your answers to these exercises. When you have done so, decide whether you wish to change any of your answers to Questions 1–7. Then check your answers to Reading Passage 1 in the Key.

READING PASSAGE 2

*You should spend about 20 minutes on **Questions 14–27**, which are based on Reading Passage 2 below.*

Play is at the heart of creative learning

A Wander into a classroom for very young children anywhere in the country, and the chances are that you'll see children at play: making things out of dough (a mixture of flour and water), putting on dressing-up clothes or playing around with sand. It may look to outsiders as if the children are just having fun, but teachers and psychologists know that play is how children learn. Through play, they become mini-scientists, exploring the world around them. But they also learn social skills and teamwork, and discover what can occur when they let their imaginations run free.

B If it's so good for very young children, why do we stop encouraging play as they move up the school? According to a recent survey by LEGO® Education, an education provider, teachers believe that greater use of creative approaches is needed in the classroom to help students acquire essential skills for the future, and that the current curriculum, with its emphasis on teaching to the test, doesn't do enough to help creativity develop.

C A recent round-table discussion organized by *The Guardian* newspaper in the United Kingdom brought together experts from education, academia and industry to discuss how we could encourage creativity and the greater use of play in the classroom.

D So what is creative learning – and why is it important? One participant provided an explanation early on in the debate: 'Creativity comes as a result of trial and error, cooperation, curiosity, being fearless and experimenting'. To promote creativity, he argued, teachers need to shift from a 'broadcast' model of education and allow children a degree of freedom to make discoveries for themselves.

E The round table heard that schools' current emphasis on learning things by heart was failing to equip students for the world of work. One participant pointed out that what engineers often do at work is also 'play': they investigate a problem with a machine, for example, by 'playing' with it. They start with a concrete problem, then think in abstract terms about how to solve it (perhaps by building a model or writing an equation), and then apply the abstract solution to the concrete problem. An education based on learning facts or doing things by the book is no preparation for this, he argued.

F   Not all participants agreed, however, that schools are trapped in an old-fashioned 'chalk-and-talk' model of education, and some pointed out that many teachers do their best to encourage creative approaches. 'There are teachers who are desperate to open up their classrooms to more innovative kinds of ideas, but that is quite hard when there is a specific programme to follow,' the round table heard.

G   There was a view around the table that current methods of assessment were hostile to creative learning. 'The reality is that every six weeks children are tested and assessed to achieve certain goals, which are not necessarily to do with being creative or innovative. Our kids today are terrified of taking risks, of getting something wrong,' said one participant. Participants agreed that assessment and measurement of performance needed to shift away from a reliance on learning by heart and towards an emphasis on independent thinking. In Denmark, for example, a pilot scheme was introduced four years ago to allow students to use the internet in public examinations: 'The moment you begin to go down that road, you stop the potential for an examination only being about reciting facts.'

H   On the basis that, as one participant put it, 'what you measure is what you will get', there was a suggestion that creativity could itself be included as a measure for evaluating schools – although one participant argued that the idea of measurement weakened the very notion of creativity: 'I fear better measurement of creativity would restrain teachers and learners in being creative.'

I   What practical approaches can teachers take to promote creativity within the classroom? The key was to move away from seeing the teacher as an authority figure, the round table agreed. 'The very first thing that needs to change is that pupils need to be encouraged to question the teacher,' said one participant. 'As soon as you get an interaction, you move towards cooperation, and the potential for creativity.'

J   Another participant argued that any genuinely creative approach to learning had to include the 'three As': authenticity, autonomy and ambiguity. 'Authenticity is about solving real-world problems, and that drives motivation and brings relevance to what you're learning. Autonomy is about giving the child the ability to solve the problem their own way and explore their own idea. Ambiguity is about allowing a level of risk, that you have uncertainty about how you solve the problem. The challenge in teaching is the correct level of support for the child, so it's not too risky, but there is sufficient ambiguity.'

Questions 14–20

Reading Passage 2 has ten paragraphs, A–J.

Which paragraph contains the following information?

NB You may use any letter more than once.

14 a reference to the likely activities in a classroom for those in the first years of school

15 a definition of creative learning

16 a reference to the frequency of assessment

17 a description of working methods used in one profession

18 the fact that children are reluctant to make mistakes

19 the question of whether creativity should be used to assess schools

20 the teachers' view that there is a necessity for more creative methods in the classroom

Questions 21–24

Complete the sentences below.

*Choose **NO MORE THAN THREE WORDS** from the passage for each answer.*

21 Apart from skills acquisition and learning about teamwork, play allows children to see
    what happens once their ....

22 In the modern school curriculum, teaching .... is stressed rather than creativity.

23 One view advocated encouraging creativity by moving away from a ....
    of education.

24 Some participants thought that far from hindering creativity, teachers are .... to
    introduce innovation.

Questions 25–27

*Choose the correct letter, **A**, **B**, **C** or **D**.*

25 In the scheme described in paragraph G, internet use in exams
    A prevented tests being only about reproducing facts.
    B led the education system down a dangerous road.
    C encouraged widespread cheating in the test.
    D stopped children from learning essential facts.

26 According to one participant's view in paragraph I, creativity can be reached if pupils
    A learn to tell the teacher what to do.
    B are given more control in the classroom.
    C interact more with the teacher.
    D are taught more computer science.

27 According to the participant's explanation in paragraph J, in creative learning autonomy
    is about
    A children working out problems with their peers.
    B giving children freedom to learn for themselves.
    C allowing children to take risks to solve problems.
    D playing games in the classroom that involve problem-solving.

Before you check your answers to Reading Passage 2, go to pages 24–25.

Questions 14–20: Matching information

The phrases in matching tasks can relate to a detail in a paragraph, part of a paragraph or a whole paragraph.

The questions below and on page 25 will help you to make sure you have chosen the correct answers for Questions 14–20 in Reading Passage 2.

Question 14 *Look at paragraph A and answer the questions below.*

1 Does the first sentence of the paragraph mention the word *classroom*?

....

2 What does the phrase *the chances are* mean?

....

3 What activities are mentioned in the first sentence?

....

....

Question 15 *Look at paragraph D and answer the questions below.*

1 What is the purpose of this paragraph? Which sentence is this likely to be in?

....

....

2 How much of the paragraph relates to an explanation?

....

....

3 What other word do you know which has a similar meaning to *explanation*?

....

Question 16 *Look at paragraph G and answer the questions below.*

1 Write down a phrase in the second sentence that indicates frequency.

....

2 In paraphrasing, other forms of a word are sometimes used, e.g. an adjective or a noun. These words form a word family. It is important to learn to notice words related to each other in this way. Which word in the paragraph is related to the word 'assessment'?

....

Question 17 *Look at paragraph E and answer the questions below.*

1 What does the writer want to do in this paragraph: describe a process or give examples?

....

2 Does the second sentence mention a profession? If so, what is it?

....

3 Do any of the words in the paragraph show that steps in a process are being described? How many steps are described?

....

....

4 Are the steps related to work?

....

Question 18 *Read the rubric for the task. Look at paragraph G again and answer the questions below.*

1 Which word in the paragraph is a synonym of *children*?

....

2 Does the word *terrified* mean something positive or negative?

....

3 Is the phrase *taking risks, of getting something wrong* related to making mistakes?

....

Question 19 *Look at paragraph H and answer the questions below.*

1 Why did the writer write this paragraph?

....

....

2 Does the paragraph contain any words related to recommendation or proposal? Which words?

....

3 Look at the second line. Which words relate to 'being used'?

....

4 Which word relates to 'assessing'?

....

5 Does the paragraph indicate that the suggestion is accepted by everyone?

....

Question 20 *Look at paragraph B and answer the questions below.*

1 Is the view of people other than the writer's expressed in the second sentence? If so, whose?

....

2 Does the paragraph mention that some things need to be used more? If so, what things? Where do they need to be used?

....

3 What other words do you know related to the word *needed*? What synonyms do you know?

....

....

Now check your answers to these exercises. When you have done so, decide whether you wish to change any of your answers to Questions 14–20. Then check your answers to Reading Passage 2 in the Key.

READING PASSAGE 3

55

*You should spend about 20 minutes on **Questions 28–40**, which are based on Reading Passage 3 below.*

Why 'singing' sand dunes hum certain notes

What does Elvis Presley have in common with a sand dune? No, it's not that people sometimes spot both in the neighbourhood of Las Vegas. Instead, some sand dunes, like Presley, can sing. And new research looking for evidence of how streams of sand can sing may explain why some dunes do it in more than one sound at the same time.

Sand dunes only sing in a few areas across the globe, and their songs – always a low, dull sound – have been an object of curiosity for centuries. Marco Polo encountered their ghostly song during his travels and Charles Darwin, in his book *The Voyage of the Beagle*, wrote of witness reports from Chileans about the sound of a sandy hill they called the 'bellower'. The song of the sands is a low hum. These dunes only sing when the sand is sliding down their sides. People can set the sand in motion themselves or, more creepily, the wind can create avalanches or landslides, producing a sudden, loud chorus.

Scientists previously thought the sound arose because avalanching sand created vibrations in the more stable layers of sand inside the dunes. But evidence that the avalanche of sand itself sings, not the dunes, emerged from experiments in 2009 by researchers who made a shallow pile of sand sing while spilling down a laboratory slope. Now, the same research team has investigated a deeper mystery of the dunes – how multiple notes can sound at the same time from one dune.

To study this question, physicist Simon Dagois-Bohy and his fellow researchers at Paris Diderot University in France recorded two different dunes: one in south-western Morocco, and one in south-eastern Oman. No matter where recordings were made near the Moroccan dune, the sands sang consistently at about 105 hertz. The Omani sands also sang powerfully, but sometimes released many different sounds of almost every possible frequency from 90 to 150 hertz.

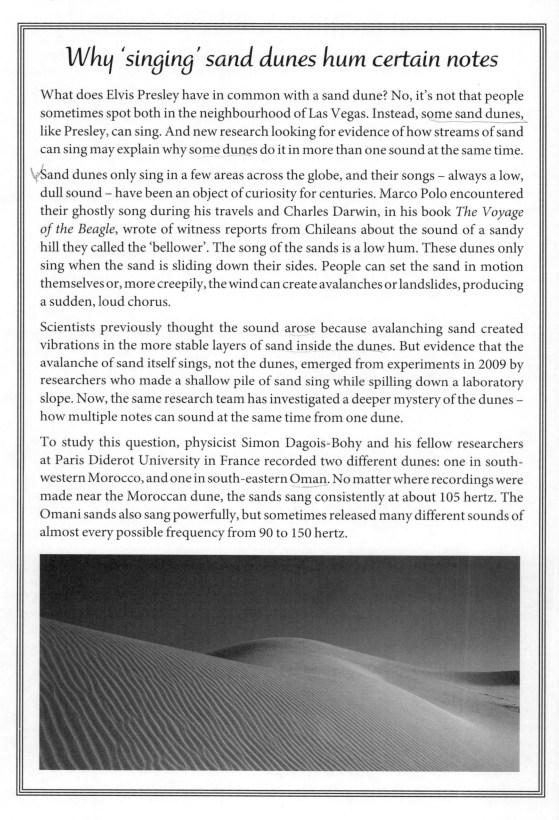

Even though the Omani dunes are not very good singers, the researchers identified some tones that were slightly stronger than others. But with all the sand avalanching at once, those noticeable frequencies were often buried in a large number of notes. The scientists also observed that sand grains from the Omani dune came in a much wider range of sizes than the Moroccan: the Omani dune's grains were 150 to 310 microns, while the Moroccan dune's grains were only 150 to 170 microns.

So Dagois-Bohy and his colleagues brought grains from the Omani dune back to the lab. First, they ran the mix of the Omani sands down a constructed slope, recording its sound with microphones and calculating the sand's vibrations with sensors that floated on the surface. Then, they isolated the sand grains that were between 200 and 250 microns, and ran those sands down the same slope.

The researchers then compared the sound of the isolated sands with the sound of the mixed-size control. They found that while the grains of a broad size range sang noisily, the sands of a narrow size range sang a clear note at about 90 hertz, much like the Moroccan sands do naturally. 'This suggested that grain size is of some significance in the tone the dunes sing in,' Dagois-Bohy said.

The research team suggests the grain size affects the purity of sounds generated by the dunes. When grain size varies, the streams of sand flow at varied speeds, producing a wider range of notes. When the grains of sand are all about the same size, the streams of sand within the avalanche move at more consistent speeds. This causes the sound to narrow in on specific tones. 'But scientists still don't know how the irregular motion of flowing grains translates into sounds coherent enough to sound like musical notes,' Dagois-Bohy said.

'The study attempts, and I think succeeds in many ways, to solve the problem of what the mechanism is that translates falling sand into a song,' said Tom Patitsas, a theoretical physicist at Laurentian University in Sudbury, Ontario, who did not participate in the study. Patitsas said the theory behind the sound still requires more explanation as to why, for example, the flowing sand still needs a thin layer of stationary sand underneath it to make a sound. He suggests the flowing sands vibrate with similar-sized grains beneath the avalanche. Those grains may lie in chain-like patterns that intensify the vibration. 'Once you have this, the sound volume of the vibration will be large,' Patitsas said.

*

Questions 28–32

Do the following statements agree with the claims of the writer in Reading Passage 3?

Write

YES   *if the statement agrees with the claims of the writer*
NO   *if the statement contradicts the claims of the writer*
NOT GIVEN   *if it is impossible to say what the writer thinks about this*

28 All sand dunes sing in different tones simultaneously.

29 Singing sand dunes are not common around the world.

30 Only the wind can make the sand dunes sing.

31 In the past, it was believed that the sound of the singing sands came from within the dunes.

32 The sound produced by the sand grains in the Omani dunes is thought to be unique.

Questions 33–37

Complete the summary using the list of words, A–J, below.

Lab experiments on the Omani sand

A test was carried out on grains from the Omani sand dune in a **33** .... After building a slope, researchers poured a mix of the Omani sands down it. The sound was recorded with microphones and the **34** .... were measured with sensors. At the next stage, the sand grains that were **35** .... in size were separated out and were then run down the same slope. A **36** .... of the sound of both types of sand were made. The results suggested that grain size is **37** .... in the tone of the song of sand dunes.

A an important factor	**B** sound	**C** of little significance
D between 200 and 250 microns	**E** detailed analysis	**F** laboratory
G between 150 to 170 microns	**H** sand's vibrations	**I** comparison
J size of sand grains		

Questions 38–40

Answer the questions below.

*Choose **NO MORE THAN TWO WORDS** from the passage for each answer.*

38 According to Patitsas, what is still lacking in the theory related to sound made by sand?

39 What does Patitsas say is needed beneath sliding sand to cause vibrations?

40 What, according to Patitsas, is increased if the vibration is intensified?

Now check your answers to Reading Passage 3.

Academic Writing 60 minutes
WRITING TASK 1

You should spend about 20 minutes on this task.

> *The graphs below show the percentage of households with internet and broadband access in Australia, together with frequency of internet access, between 2006–07 and 2012–13.*
>
> *Summarize the information by selecting and reporting the main features, and make comparisons where relevant.*

Write at least 150 words.

Households with internet and broadband access

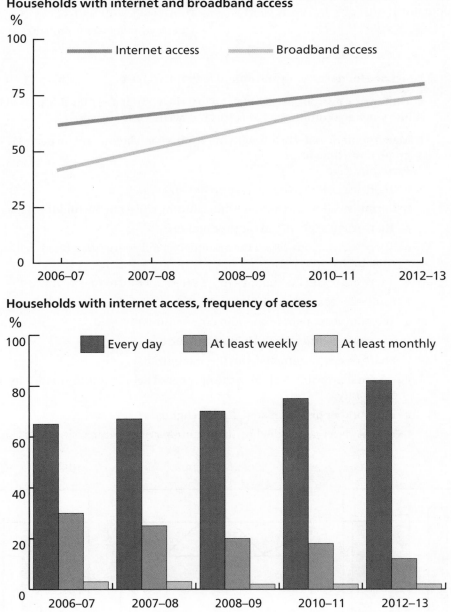

Households with internet access, frequency of access

Before you write your answer to Writing Task 1, go to pages 30–32.

Tips

Writing Task 1

- Make sure you do Writing Task 1 first and spend no more than 20 minutes on writing your answer.
- Read the rubric and study the data, etc carefully.
- Note the word 'Summarize' in the rubric.
- Make notes on the diagram itself and number the points you are going to write about in order.
- Remember you need to write about all the information. However, you should not just list the information, but summarize it.
- Paraphrase the rubric as the word count will start after the introduction if you copy the rubric word for word.

- Make sure you write an overview of all of the data.
- Use a wide range of vocabulary and grammatical structures.
- Combine information using complex sentences and remember to compare and contrast data.
- Take care with the tenses.
- Make sure you write in paragraphs.
- Do not write less than the word limit as this will affect your score band. There is no upper limit, but aim for about 180 words maximum. Remember, the rubric says 'summarize'.
- Check your answer for mistakes.

Language for describing movement in graphs/charts

The following exercises will help you to write your answer for this part of the test. When you have completed Exercises 1–4, write your answer.

1 Match sentences **a–l** below with the graphs **i–viii** below and on page 31. You may use any graph more than once.
Example: **a** *viii*

a There was a sharp rise in the purchase of iWatches.

b Furniture sales were rather erratic, hitting a peak in the middle of the period.

c There was a slight dip in car production.

d There was a steady rise in the amount of wind energy generated, followed by a period of stability.

e There were wild fluctuations in TV sales, but the trend was upward.

f Fruit sales rose dramatically.

g The number of people attending the lectures plunged.

h There was a dramatic fall in the share price.

i Share prices plummeted, but then stabilized.

j After a significant decline in the number of people settling in the city, there was a period of stability.

k The number of houses sold dipped slightly.

l There was a gradual decline in the number of children visiting the zoo.

i

ii

iii

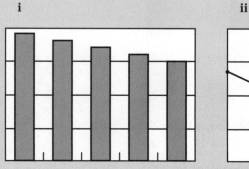
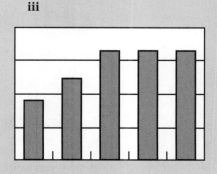

iv

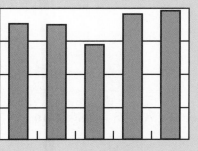

v

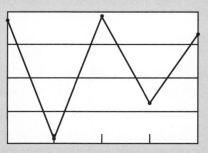

vi

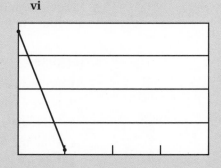

vii

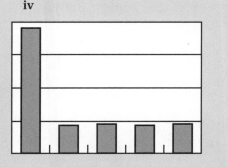

viii

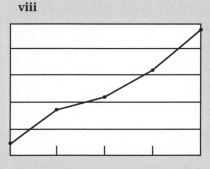

2 Is it possible to rewrite sentences **a–e** on page 30 as they are written below?

a *Purchases of iWatches rose sharply over the period.*

b *There were fluctuations in the sale of furniture, with sales reaching a high in the middle of the period.*

c *Car production dipped slightly.*

d *The amount of wind energy generated rose steadily, followed by a period of stability.*

e *TV sales fluctuated wildly, but the trend was upward.*

3 Rewrite sentences **f–l**. Which verb in the sentences cannot be changed into a noun?

4 Look at the bar chart on page 29. Add phrases **a–f** below to complete the noun phrases in each sentence. There may be more than one answer in each sentence.

a weekly access or more
b daily access to the internet
c those accessing the internet at least once a week

d monthly access or more
e those accessing the internet monthly
f those accessing the internet on a daily basis

1 The trend for ....*d/e*............ was flat.

2 The trend for .... was downward.

3 The trend for .... was upward.

4 There was a significant rise in the proportion of ....

5 There was little change in .... throughout the period.

6 The proportion of .... declined.

7 The trend in .... to the internet fell gradually.

8 .... to the internet fell.

9 The proportion of .... increased signifantly.

10 .... remained flat throughout the period.

Now check your answers to these exercises. When you have finished, go to page 32.

5 Now write your answer to Writing Task 1 on page 29. When you have finished, use the questions in the Checklist below to help you check your answer.

Checklist

1 Is the answer at least 150 words?

2 Is the answer divided into paragraphs? How many?

3 Does the answer summarize the information or list it?

4 Does the introduction paraphrase or copy the rubric?

5 Is there a clear overview summarizing all the data?

6 Is all the relevant data included in the answer?

7 Is there a clear link between the two sets of data?

8 Is there a wide range of vocabulary to avoid repetition?

9 Are there examples of complex sentences?
   Give an example.

10 Are there any mistakes in the answer?

6 Now look at the possible answer for Writing Task 1 below and answer questions **1–10** above.

The charts provide information about the proportion of Australian households that have access to the internet along with the frequency of access between 2006–07 and 2012–13.

As regards general internet access, broadband and non-broadband, the proportion of households grew gradually from approximately 70% to around 77% in 2006–07 and 2012–13 respectively. By comparison, broadband access climbed at a faster pace up to 2010–11, going up from about 40% to 68% respectively, while the rise in the latter period mirrored the overall access with an increase to about 74%.

There seems to be a correlation between the increase in access and the frequency of internet access. The proportion of those accessing the internet daily rose from about 63% to 83%. By contrast, although there was a steady decline in access at least once per week from around 30% to 20%, the trend in access at least once a month remained flat (approximately 1%).

Overall, there is a clear upward trend in internet access and internet use with the proportion of those with broadband access on the rise.

Now check your answer to this exercise and compare it with the possible answers on page 132. Then do Writing Task 2 on page 33.

WRITING TASK 2

You should spend about 40 minutes on this task.

Write about the following topic:

> *Some people believe that parents should be responsible for encouraging their children to take regular exercise. Others argue that the main responsibility for encouraging children to do so should lie with schools.*
>
> *Discuss both these views and give your own opinion.*

Give reasons for your answer and include any relevant examples from your own knowledge or experience.

Write at least 250 words.

When you have written your answer to Task 2, compare it with the possible answers on pages 132–133.

Speaking 11–14 minutes

PART 1 INTRODUCTION AND INTERVIEW (4–5 MINUTES)

In this part, the examiner will check your identification and you will introduce yourself. He/She will ask you about yourself, your home, work or studies and other familiar topics.

Example

Hobbies

- What hobbies are popular in your country? [Why?]
- Do you have any hobbies? [Why/Why not?]
- How do you think your hobbies are different to those of your parents? [Why?]
- Do you think it is important for young people nowadays to have hobbies? [Why/Why not?]

Before you practise the task, go to the Further Practice and Guidance section on page 35.

PART 2 TASK CARD (3–4 MINUTES)

Describe a time when someone helped you.

You should say:
> who the person was
> where and when the person helped you
> what the person did to help you
> and explain how you felt when the person helped you.

You will have to talk about the topic for one to two minutes.
You have one minute to think about what you are going to say.
You can make some notes to help you if you wish.

Before you practise the task, go to the Further Practice and Guidance section on page 35.

PART 3 DISCUSSION (4–5 MINUTES)

Discussion topics:

Importance of helping people

Example questions:

- Do you think it is important to have friends to help in times of trouble? Why/Why not?
- Why do some people volunteer to help others? Is this suitable for everyone?
- Some say that people helped each other more in the past. Do you agree? Why?

International help

Example questions:

- Do you think it is a good idea to use famous people to draw attention to international issues? Why/Why not?
- How do international organizations give help in your country?
- What is the best way for young people to learn about the importance of helping others? Why?

Tips

Part 1: Introduction and interview

- Relax during the Speaking component of the test.
- Follow the examiner's instructions and be sensitive to turn-taking in Part 1.
- Answer the questions in Part 1 by giving one or two sentences for your answer rather than one or two words.
- Give reasons and examples from your personal experience.
- Be prepared for a wide range of familiar topics, not just those related to your family and friends.
- Speak fluently at a natural speed. This does not mean you should speak fast.

The questions aim to help you relax so that you can begin to speak naturally. In Part 1 on page 34, the questions are about hobbies. You need to give answers that are more than one or two words, but no more than one or two sentences.

1 To prepare to answer questions on different familiar topics, make notes about the items below, where possible.

Topics	Hobbies	Family	Studying	Ambition	Buildings
Examples					
Reasons					
Frequency					
Vocabulary					

2 Write one possible question for each of the topics in the table.

Now check your answers to these exercises.

Tips

Part 2: Task card

- Make notes for each prompt on the paper provided.
- Write no more than 10–12 words.
- Write the words in the order of the prompts.
- Arrange the words so that you can glance at them as you speak without having to work out the order.
- Avoid complicated diagrams as there isn't time to create them.
- Make sure you connect your ideas and develop the last prompt fully.
- Aim to speak for one to two minutes. The examiner will then ask you a few questions to link Part 2 to Part 3.

In the test, you will have paper and a pencil to make notes. It is important you use the minute to write short notes to help you organize your answer.

Write no more than 10–12 words below to help you prepare to talk about the task card on page 34.

Time: .... *teenager* ....

Person: ....

Place: ....

Help: ....

How I felt: ....

Think briefly about your notes, deciding how you can talk about each one.

Then, talk about the topic on the task card on page 34. Remember you can look quickly at your notes as you speak.

Test 2

30 D

Listening approximately 30 minutes

SECTION 1 *Questions 1–10* 🎧 1.20–1.25

Questions 1–10

Complete the notes below.

*Write **NO MORE THAN TWO WORDS AND/OR A NUMBER** for each answer.*

Insurance enquiry

Example

Information on: ....*health*.......

Name: Daniella Forbes

Insurance: for the **1** ..whole family.. for one year

Ages

- Boy: 7 years old
- Girl: **2** .....9..... years old
- Husband: 31 years old
- Wife: 33 years old

Occupations

- Husband: **3** primary school teacher
- Wife: lecturer

Health in the past

- No previous **4** .....injury..... in the family

Health plan

- cover for dentist, optician, doctor and **5** hospital stays
- also covers: **6** .... therapies including acupuncture and physiotherapy

Cost

- **7** £ .....70.69..... per month

Reference number: 8 .....PB663885FJ.....

Discount: first **9** .....2 months..... free

Payment: one year **10** ..in advance.. or monthly installments

---

Stop the recording when you hear 'That is the end of Section 1.'

Now check your answers to Section 1 of the test.

SECTION 2 *Questions 11–20* 🎧 1.26–1.30

Questions 11–13

Choose THREE letters, A–G.

Which **THREE** attractions in the town does the speaker mention?

The town of St John's

A famous shops

B a local museum

C fast-food restaurants

D bookshops ✓

E a golf course ✓

F a film festival

G coffee shops ✓

Questions 14–17

What comments does the speaker make about each of the beaches?

*Choose **FOUR** answers from the box and write the correct letter, A–G, next to questions 14–17.*

> A appropriate for families
> B several facilities
> C extremely beautiful
> D attractive to surfers
> E difficult for parking
> F popular in winter
> G full of cafés

14 Black Rock   ....E........ ✓

15 Sandy Beach   ....A........ ✓

16 Port Tray   ....D........ ✓

17 Little Cove   ....C........ ✓

Questions 18–20

Complete the notes below.

*Write **NO MORE THAN TWO WORDS** for each answer.*

In the countryside, tourists can also

- go to villages to see **18** ....old houses.... ✓
- enjoy coastal walks on the cliff tops
- explore **19** ....woodland.... - with facilities for picnics ✓
- take part in water sports such as **20** ....canoeing.... and ....swimming....

Stop the recording when you hear 'That is the end of Section 2.'

Now check your answers to Section 2 of the test.

SECTION 3 *Questions 21–30* 🎧 1.31–1.35

Questions 21–23

Answer the questions below.

*Write **NO MORE THAN THREE WORDS** for each answer.*

21 Which commodity did Tanya first plan to focus on?

....~~sugar~~.... *[handwritten: future]*

22 Which two commodities did Carlo think Tanya was focusing on in her seminar?

....*metals and oil* ✓....

23 What is the cause of corn price increases that Tanya mentions?

....*population growth* ✓....

Questions 24–27

Complete the table below.

*Write **NO MORE THAN ONE WORD OR A NUMBER** for each answer.*

Corn exporters

Country	Ranking	Volume	Comments
United States	1st	513,834 million tonnes	– 36% of world corn production – About 24 ....*50*.... % more in 10 years' time
United Kingdom	3rd	25 ....*114*.... million tonnes	EU – 3% of world corn production
Chile	5th	6 million tonnes	Latin America – huge 26 ....*potential*.... Approximately 27 ....*40* ✓.... % of world's uncultivated cropland

Questions 28–30

Complete the sentences below.

*Write **NO MORE THAN TWO WORDS AND/OR A NUMBER** for each answer.*

28 Tanya says she will have difficulty speaking without a ....*read script*....

29 Carlo limits the time he speaks for each slide to ....*2 minutes* ✓....

30 The tutor says it is fine for Carlo to use ....*special feature*.... on his slides. ✓

Stop the recording when you hear 'That is the end of Section 3.'

Before you check your answers to Section 3 of the test, go to pages 39–40.

Tips

Questions 21–23: Answering questions

- Circle the word limit in the rubric.
- Skim the questions and check the names.
- Think of who might give the information in the answers.
- Underline the question word and the key words to listen for.

- Predict the type of word that is required and a possible answer. Even if your prediction is wrong, it will help you listen for the answer in the Listening test.
- Predict where possible answers that might have one, two or three words.
- When you answer questions about facts, it is important to use the structure of the questions to help you.

Underline the correct word or phrase below in italics to make true statements about Questions 21-23 on page 38.

Question 21

The words 'Which commodity' are likely to mean that the answer has *one/two/three* word(s). The answer is a(n) *noun/adjective/verb/adverb*. The answer is *less/more* likely to be a noun phrase as most commodities are one word. Tanya is *likely/unlikely* to mention a word/phrase related to 'first'.

Question 22

The answer has at least two *nouns/adjectives/verbs/adverbs* and is likely to contain the word *and/or/with*, because the rubric allows you to write three words. The change of speaker from Tanya to Carlo *doesn't help/helps* you to find the answer.

Question 23

The words 'What is the cause of … price increases' mean that the answer is likely to be a *noun phrase or noun/noun or adjective/verb or adverb*. If it's a noun phrase, it's unlikely to be *an adjective + a noun/a noun + a noun/a noun + a preposition + a noun*. Again, the change of speaker from Carlo to Tanya *doesn't help/helps* you to find the answer.

Questions 24–27: Following a table

Note that the table needs to be read from left to right horizontally. The position of the questions also helps you to find your way around the table. To see the patterns of the answers, however, the columns need to be read vertically.

Use the structure of the table and the other information to help you answer questions **1–10** below and on page 40. Circle the correct answer.

1 Do Questions 24-26 show you which direction to read the table?

   yes | no

2 In which direction is the information presented in the recording?

   horizontally | vertically

3 Do you use the headings in bold to follow the information as it is provided?

   yes | no

4 Does the answer for Question 24 come after the volume and the percentage 36%?

yes | no

5 What is the answer for Question 24 likely to be?

a number | a noun

6 What clues are there for the answer to Question 24 in the *Comments* column?

nouns | percentages

7 What is the likely answer for Question 25?

A much *smaller | larger* number than for the USA

8 Do the percentages for the USA and the EU in the *Comments* column help you answer Question 25?

yes | no

9 What is the answer for Question 26?

a noun | a number

10 What is the answer for Question 27?

a noun | a number

Questions 28–30: Completing sentences

Always try to think of possible correct answers. Do you agree with the statements below?

Question 28
The answer has to be something that Tanya reads, holds or looks at briefly.

....

Question 29
It is likely that the answer is in minutes, because 'seconds' is too short and 'hours' is too long.

....

Question 30
The answer is likely to be about something that the slides have (colour/quotes/pictures/large font) or do (change/transform in some way).

....

Now check your answers to these tasks. When you have done so, listen to Section 3 again and decide whether you wish to change any of your original answers. Then check your answers to Section 3 of the test.

SECTION 4 *Questions 31–40* 🎧 1.36–1.38

Questions 31–34

Choose the correct letter, A, B or C.

The University Fashion Design Project

31 The government gave money to the Fashion Design Project to

    A expand the department's research facilities.
    B help build external commercial links.
    C promote the Fashion Department externally.

32 Collaboration with other departments and outside companies has increased the

    A attractiveness of the products to customers.
    B number of young people involved in the design process.
    C variety of products that can be produced.

33 Raising the profile of the Fashion Department has resulted in

    A small cuts in government support.
    B alarm in the wider fashion industry.
    C more money for research purposes.

34 Early design prototypes of wearable technology didn't function properly, because

    A the fabrics in the vests and shirts tore easily.
    B the models felt the clothes were too simple in design.
    C the technology did not work well with the clothes.

Questions 35–40

Complete the notes below.

Write **ONE WORD ONLY** *for each answer.*

Fashion items

Focus on

- other **35** .... , e.g. bracelets
- attraction of items to general public
- design not just **36** ....function....

Challenges

- Main challenge: public may not want technology in their clothes
  – extra cost possibly off-putting
- Need to create clothes that work, get the attention of the public and
  are **37** ...inexpensive...
- People possibly technology-weary
  – introduction of product into the market at the appropriate **38** ...advirtesity...
- Using appealing **39** ....

Possible drawbacks

- Possible obsession with data
- Not leave home without tech-wearables
- Destruction of clothes and technology through **40** ......cleaning.......

Stop the recording when you hear 'That is the end of Section 4.'

Before you check your answers to Section 4 of the test, go to pages 43–44.

Tips

Questions 31–34: Multiple-choice questions

Understanding some common patterns in multiple-choice questions can help prepare you to answer them efficiently.

- Listen carefully to the instructions which will describe the overall contents of this section.
- Look at any headings or subheadings.
- Skim all the questions as you only have 40 seconds to read them at the beginning and a five-second pause before Questions 35–40.
- Work out the relationship between the stem of the multiple-choice questions and the options.

- Look for key words in the stem and the options and think of synonyms, paraphrases of words and different ways of using grammar structures.
- As you listen, pay attention to various words that may be in the same word family, e.g. *access, accessible.*
- Concentrate throughout as the answers can be *close together* or *far apart.*

1 Use the checklist below to examine the stems and the options in Questions 31–34. Circle the answers.

Multiple-choice question checklist

Question 31

1	Is the verb in the stem passive?	*Yes | No*
2	Do the options each contain a purpose?	*Yes | No*
3	Are all the purposes positive?	*Yes | No*
4	Can you rephrase the stem using the passive?	*Yes | No*

Question 32

5	Does the stem contain a cause and effect relationship?	*Yes | No*
6	Are there other ways of expressing the words in the stem?	*Yes | No*

Question 33

7	Does the stem contain a result?	*Yes | No*
8	Do the options each contain a cause?	*Yes | No*
9	Is the phrase 'result in' in the stem the same as 'result from'?	*Yes | No*

Question 34

10	Does the stem contain a cause?	*Yes | No*
11	Does the stem contain an effect?	*Yes | No*
12	Do the options each contain an effect?	*Yes | No*
13	Do the options each contain a cause?	*Yes | No*

2 What other questions could you ask? Make your own electronic version of the checklist for your tablet or mobile phone. Refine the list as you come across different multiple-choice questions.

Always remember that noticing the grammatical structures and features such as cause and effect in multiple-choice questions can help you answer the questions.

3 Look at Questions 31–34 again and identify the words and phrases in the stems and options which can be paraphrased by the items below.

a *teamwork/working together/cooperation*

b *improved reputation*

c *provided funding for*

d *a result/a consequence/because of*

e *examples*

f *difficult to get to work properly*

Questions 35–40: Completing notes

In the Listening component, you need to be able to read and *process notes very quickly*. You need to be able to understand how the information in note form fits together. This is a skill you need to become very competent in as you prepare for the IELTS test. Remember that you will hear the recording once only.

Read the notes in Questions 35–40 and expand them automatically as you read. Add general nouns such as things or items on the lines below if you can.

Example:

Question 35
The Design Project is focusing or concentrating on additional/other [things/items].
These items need to attract the public.

Question 36

....
....

Question 37

....
....

Question 38

....
....

Question 39

....
....

Question 40

....
....

Now check your answers to these tasks. When you have done so, listen to Section 4 again and decide whether you wish to change any of your original answers. Then check your answers to Section 4 of the test.

Academic Reading 60 minutes

READING PASSAGE 1

*You should spend about 20 minutes on **Questions 1–13**, which are based on Reading Passage 1 on the following pages.*

Questions 1–5

Reading Passage 1 has seven paragraphs, **A–G**.

*Choose the correct heading for paragraphs **B–F** from the list of headings below.*

List of Headings

i	The relationship between two qualities that drive success
ii	The need to be able to see any project through to the end
iii	Strategies to develop self-motivation
iv	Two attributes that people can acquire
v	The ability to see and act on possibilities before others
vi	The qualities necessary for success in the modern world
vii	A comparison between talent and ambition
viii	The possibility that being flexible is the most important attribute
ix	The need for qualities other than just knowledge and skills

---

Example	Answer
Paragraph **A**	**ix**

1 Paragraph **B**

2 Paragraph **C**

3 Paragraph **D**

4 Paragraph **E**

5 Paragraph **F**

Example	Answer
Paragraph **G**	**viii**

Young people – what do they need for success today?

A Having knowledge and skills seems to overshadow the debate about what young people need to equip themselves for success in life, academically, professionally and socially. Much more than these two entities, however, now seems to be demanded of the younger generation than previously. The young are often unjustly measured by the media and parents against knowledge-focused criteria that are more relevant to previous generations than to the modern digital age. This is not to say that knowledge and skills are unimportant; they are essential. But success for young people today requires a range of attributes, some of which may be possible to teach and develop. Yet many, if not most, are innate.

B The acquisition of a good education may often be quoted as being necessary for success, but the business world is full of successful people who have had an average or little education, as are the arts and sports worlds. Being creative even at a very basic level is an attribute that to some people is much more important than education, and it is often cited as the single most important quality in success. It can be argued that being creative is not just an innate quality. Steve Jobs once said 'Creativity is about seeing connections', often that other people do not see. Just like having a good education, it seems that this noticing or seeing in creativity can be taught.

C Other attributes such as being ambitious and having talent cannot be taught, but these, like being well-educated or creative, are not enough to guarantee success. What is probably more necessary than these qualities is having a vision. This involves being able to see a finished project or product such as a website, or any business venture and seeing the various stages up to the very end, and indeed beyond. It also includes something as mundane as being able to state clear aims and objectives that can be worked back from. An idea for a project on its own is not sufficient.

D Self-motivation and perseverance are further strengths which are inextricably linked and are necessary to 'develop a vision'. These are essential forces that propel successful people, if they are to initiate a project, to stay the course and take it to the end. Being self-motivated, for example, enables people to start up a business web page, or design an app. Perseverance then enables someone to keep going in the face of criticism and obstacles. It is difficult to separate the two qualities, as both are needed to keep going even in the face of failure. However, it can be difficult for people to pick themselves up and continue when they have a setback and become upset. Being able to examine failure, and analyse, tolerate and use it is an important part of both self-motivation and perseverance. In fact, failure is useful because it can help sharpen people's talents, especially once they have learnt how it can be dealt with. It is doubtful whether self-motivation and perseverance can themselves be taught, but people with and without these qualities try to use a range of techniques.

E People can be very disciplined and organized, which is useful in self-motivation, but sometimes it is also worth having something positive to look forward to. This simple technique of bribing oneself can consist of everyday things such as chocolate or sweets, or a relaxing activity, even something as basic as going for a walk or reading a newspaper. Self-motivation can also be initiated by limiting the time spent working on something, for example two hours in the morning. A golden rule is to stop working on a project when the feeling is positive. Then there is a good possibility that the work will be approached once again with eagerness and pleasure. Conversely, if work is stopped when someone is feeling negative, negativity may then be present when the work is started again. So it's wise to stop or take a break when one is in a good mood!

F Part of self-motivation is being proactive rather than reactive, that is doing things first rather than responding to other people's actions. There is a tendency generally for people to wait for someone else to initiate something new, whereas successful people are able to see opportunities, and seize them before anyone else realizes they are there. They are independent and start things on their own.

G Education, knowledge and skills may play an important part in helping people to succeed, but it is clear that other attributes such as having a vision, self-motivation and being proactive, which are less tangible and therefore difficult to quantify, are important for success. Yet, perhaps, an attribute that is more critical than any other is the ability to be flexible, as young people shift from one attribute to another, without thinking.

Glossary: *innate*: having (something) from birth

Questions 6–10

Do the following statements agree with the views of the writer in Reading Passage 1?

Write

YES	*if the statement agrees with the views of the writer*
NO	*if the statement contradicts the views of the writer*
NOT GIVEN	*if it is impossible to say what the writer thinks about this*

6 The youth of today are unfairly judged against outdated standards.

7 The necessary attributes for being successful can be learnt.

8 Being creative is a much less important factor in success than education.

9 Talent is an invaluable quality that can be nourished.

10 Failure can help people improve their talents.

Questions 11–13

Complete the sentences below.

*Choose **TWO WORDS** from the passage for each answer.*

11 According to Steve Jobs, being creative is related to ....

12 Having the ability to .... is an essential aspect of self-motivation and perseverance.

13 People should stop working when they are in a .... rather than when they are feeling negative.

Before you check your answers to Reading Passage 1, go to pages 48–49.

Tips

You may be asked to match headings to paragraphs or to sections which contain more than one paragraph. Remember that the heading must be a summary or overview of the whole paragraph or section.

- Look at the title of the reading passage.
- Read any examples (note that examples are not always given).
- Do not cross out the examples as they help you find the other headings. Write the letter for the paragraph next to the relevant heading in the list and make sure you read them.
- Skim all the headings. Circle the general nouns, e.g. *relationship*, *effect*, and underline the key words in the rest of each heading.

- Think about possible synonyms of words in the headings.
- Then skim the passage. (Alternatively, you can skim the title of the passage and the passage first.)
- When you have finished the task, read through the headings and the title and check if the order of your headings makes sense.
- As you answer the questions in the following tasks, use the headings to help you locate information. You can also use the other questions to confirm your choice of headings.

In headings, learn to see patterns such as the use of noun phrases which are created around a general noun such as *relationship, effect, solution* and so on. Keep a list of these words, as they occur in the exam again and again. Think of synonyms for them and think how they are paraphrased, e.g. *measures* may be expressed as a clause beginning '*how ...*'.

Which other general nouns can be used for the following examples in the headings on page 45?

relationship: ....
....

need: ....
....

strategies: ....
....

ability: ....
....

Now answer the following questions about the paragraphs themselves.

Paragraph B

a Are two attributes mentioned in the paragraph? If so, what are they?

....

b Look back at paragraph A. Does the end of the paragraph make a distinction between taught and innate attributes? If so, which words show this?

....

c Does the order of the words *taught* and *innate* indicate that 'taught' attributes will be looked at first?

....

d Does the last sentence of paragraph B indicate that creativity can be acquired like a good education?

....

Paragraph C

a Does the first sentence or the second sentence contain the topic of the paragraph?

....

b Which words in the two sentences indicate this?

....

c What is the purpose of the third sentence in the paragraph?

....

d Does the fourth sentence have the same purpose as the third sentence? Which words show you this?

....

Paragraph D

a Does the first sentence of paragraph D link this paragraph with paragraph C? How?

....

b What two qualities are mentioned? Where are they first mentioned?

....

c Are the two qualities linked with each other?

....

d Does the beginning of the paragraph mention anything about forces that drive successful people forward? If so, which words?

....

e Is the discussion about failure the main idea in the paragraph or just additional information?

....

Paragraph E

a Do the first two sentences mention the words *technique* and *self-motivation*?

....

b Is another technique mentioned in the paragraph? If so, which words indicate another technique is being described?

....

c Do any of the headings **i–ix** contain (a) word(s) related to techniques? If so, which ones?

....

Paragraph F

a Does the first sentence introduce a quality and explain it?

....

b What quality is mentioned?

....

c Does the second sentence contrast what other people do with the actions of successful people? If so, which words show this?

....

Now check your answers to these exercises. When you have done so, decide whether you wish to change any of your answers to Questions 1–5. Then check your answers to Reading Passage 1 in the Key.

READING PASSAGE 2

*You should spend about 20 minutes on **Questions 14–27**, which are based on Reading Passage 2 below.*

Are children consuming too much digital technology?

The popularity of apps, social networking and playing games among young people could lead to childhood development problems

How much time should children spend online or playing apps and games?

That question is one of the principal parenting challenges of our modern digital and social age. The facts about children's digital consumption are eye-opening. A 2010 Kaiser Foundation study found that US youths spent more than seven and a half hours a day using a smartphone, computer, television or other electronic device. In another study conducted that year by the Joan Ganz Cooney Centre, which specializes in children's media, two thirds of children aged four to seven had already used a smartphone. And how did these kids get hooked on digital? The Centre's own research suggests that most of the smartphones used by kids had been lent to them by a family member. As a recent *Atlantic Monthly* article put it: 'The Centre's researchers labelled this the "pass-back effect", a name that captures well the reluctant zone between denying and giving.'

Are children addicted to digital?

A mere 20 years after the internet was founded, people do not yet know how the explosion in digital connectivity is shaping society. Ever since Gutenberg's breakthrough with the movable press, each new discovery in communication technology – the telegraph, the radio, the TV and now the internet – has both been called a benefit and curse for society. Looking back in history, the benefits of all these technologies have outweighed the problems they have caused. Could it be that the world is in a new period of technological adaptation and that what is considered digital overload, or too much digital information, for children, is simply the education they need to prepare for a connected society? Perhaps. But that doesn't mean digital addiction is an issue we can just dismiss. At present there isn't a firm medical consensus on digital addiction. There are plenty of stories detailing how the internet and gaming have ruined people's lives. In South Korea, one of the most digitally advanced nations in the world, the government estimates 2.55 million people are addicted to smartphones (using them for more than eight hours a day).

While we don't know exactly the effect information overload has on people, we do know that children, especially the under-10s, are going to use digital technologies more than any generation before. Consider the apps industry that is only a few years old. According to the *Children's Technology Review*, an independent publication that monitors children's interactive media, there are more than 40,000 kids' games available on download sites on the internet. There have been cases of children running up enormous bills on their parents' credit cards due to the costs of collecting rewards in some app-based games.

How far does a company's responsibility go?

Yet even if children aren't being financially manipulated in the games, do gaming and app makers have a corporate and social responsibility to manage the impact their products have? Some companies already include warnings on their electronic games about spending too much time on their systems because of concerns about over-exertion or about the effect 3D playing has on the vision of the young. So could this principle of responsible gaming be expanded to cover digital overload as a whole? As each child and situation is unique, some feel that the decision is ultimately the responsibility of the parent, who should have a dialogue with their children on healthy digital behaviour and – as a family – set some clear rules regarding digital activity. All of which makes sense.

What about education?

Parents really should take the lead on regulating their children's digital activity and you can see why technology companies are reluctant to self-regulate against a digital affliction that has still yet to be fully understood or defined. But not all children can count on having parents who care or at this point understand the importance of managing digital health. So what role will government – or to be more exact, education – need to play in this evolving debate?

Primary age schoolkids in the UK already get some lessons in internet safety and protecting their privacy. In South Korea, however, the state education system is preparing to meet the challenge it has identified in digital obesity. Starting next year, children from ages three to five will be taught to avoid spending too much time on the internet and digital devices.

Ultimately though, how kids use digital devices and games will be dictated by the example parents set at home. This is worth considering the next time parents download an app to keep the kids quiet.

Questions 14–18

Complete the summary.

*Choose **NO MORE THAN TWO WORDS** from the passage for each answer.*

A problem for parents

The amount of time children should spend online, playing apps and games is a problem for parents and the details about digital **14** .... are quite revealing. One study showed that young people in the United States devoted nearly a third of each day to using some kind of **15** .... According to another study by an organization, which focuses on **16** .... , two thirds of all 4–7 year-olds had used a smartphone. Their research showed that this could be a result of a **17** .... lending the child the phone, aptly named the **18** .... by a recent article.

Questions 19–23

Do the following statements agree with the views of the writer in Reading Passage 2?

Write

YES	*if the statement agrees with the views of the writer*
NO	*if the statement contradicts the views of the writer*
NOT GIVEN	*if it is impossible to say what the writer thinks about this*

19 It is deeply worrying that people are unaware of the impact digital connectivity is having on society.

20 People have viewed past technologies as mainly positive.

21 It is possible that digital overload is just part of the education of children nowadays.

22 Digital addiction should not be a cause for concern.

23 The quality of apps for children is improving rapidly.

Questions 24–27

Answer the questions below.

*Choose **NO MORE THAN TWO WORDS** from the passage for each answer.*

24 Which nation is considered more digitally advanced in the way children are taught?

25 What are some companies adding to their electronic games?

26 What should parents have with their children to ensure a healthy attitude towards digital activity?

27 In the UK, what are children taught to keep safe?

Before you check your answers to Reading Passage 2, go to page 53.

Questions 14–18: Summary completion (without a wordlist)

1 Which statement below about summaries is **not** true?

    a A summary can occur with a wordlist.

    b A summary can occur with or without a title.

    c A summary with a title usually refers to part of a text.

    d Names and key words at the beginning and the end of the summary can help you to locate the information you need.

    e The information in the summary is always in the same order as it is in the text.

    f The answers in summaries are often, but not always, nouns and noun phrases.

    g Summaries with and without a title can cover the whole of a text.

    h The exact words in the reading passage need to be used in the answers.

    i The word and number limit in rubrics varies.

    j Words in the reading passage are never repeated in the summary.

2 It is useful to read through the summary thinking about the grammatical form of the answer *and* possible answers. You can then try to match your predictions with the words in the reading passage. Use the hints below to think of the missing words as you check your answers for Questions 14–18.

    Question 14 something to do with use/usage/utilization or consuming

    Question 15 items that are 'digital' or are electronic

    Question 16 something related to children that adults also use, e.g. newspapers (plural word)

    Question 17 a general word or phrase for a person in a family or other group of people

    Question 18 a name of some kind of process

3 All the answers for Questions 14–18 are nouns or noun phrases. From the hints in Exercise 2, can you predict the number of words in the answers: one word, one or two words, or two words? Or is it difficult to predict?

    14 ....

    15 ....

    16 ....

    17 ....

    18 ....

Now check your answers to these exercises. When you have done so, decide whether you wish to change any of your answers to Questions 14–18. Then check your answers to Reading Passage 2 in the Key.

READING PASSAGE 3

You should spend about 20 minutes on **Questions 28–40**, which are based on Reading Passage 3 below.

BRIDGES
OBJECTS OF BEAUTY
OR USEFULNESS?

What is the purpose of bridges? Are they just functional pieces of infrastructure, or are they objects of delight?

Bridges are among the most beautiful structures in the world, and the most useful. The latter is their main attribute as they have served mankind through the millennia bridging natural obstacles, streams, rivers, valleys, gulfs and even bays such as Hangzhou Bay Bridge in China. They serve as a testament to the ingenuity of the human race by the elegance of their structure, the materials they use, the distance they span and the purpose they serve connecting space. And architects continue to delight and astonish us with their prowess.

Roman civilization might not have spread quite so far had it not been for the Romans' ability to build not just roads, but solid bridges to carry water and armies that endure to this day. The Roman bridge was a far cry from the wooden or stone structures of the past made by our ancestors, who must have created simple bridges over streams, marshy terrain or possibly even rivers using the material that was at hand such as rocks, stones or fallen trees. It was not until the Romans introduced the arch that building bridges and aqueducts that were wider and longer became a reality, such as the Roman bridge at Alcántara in Spain that spans the River Tagus with its two massive central arches. It was only in 1779 that Darby's Iron Bridge across the River Severn in the United Kingdom, well known for being the first of its kind in the world, achieved what the Romans had hundreds of years before.

Bridges were and are built to be elegant architectural masterpieces as well as functional parts of transport infrastructure. While any selection of bridges in any country can only be subjective, few would deny that the Zhaozhou Bridge in Hebei Province in north-east China, the oldest standing bridge in China, is one of the most elegant in the world with its famous main arch and intricate engravings. Built during the Sui Dynasty (581–618 AD), the construction of the bridge took ten years, and although old it is surprisingly solid as well as supremely elegant and is surely a match for the Charles Bridge in Prague in the Czech Republic.

Modern bridges do not have to be long or large to be appealing to the eye. Across the Thames, in London, there is the Millennium Bridge, or Wobbly Bridge, as it was first known when it swayed after a large number of people crossed it at one time. There is also the Swing Bridge in Gateshead and a very elegant rolling bridge, which is a footbridge spanning an inlet of the Grand Union Canal at Paddington Basin, London, designed by Thomas Heatherwick. These are all modern bridges with great appeal.

Bridges were built with buildings on them such as old London Bridge across the River Thames, begun in the late 11th century AD. It stood for six hundred years before it was demolished and a fairly conventional five-arch stone bridge, designed by Rennie and opened in 1831, was put in its place. This later bridge was sold to an American Robert McCulloch and reconstructed again at Lake Havasu City, Arizona. It was then replaced once more with a modern structure, which opened in 1972. Another famous bridge with commercial units still along its length today is the Ponte Vecchio across the River Arno in Florence, Italy, a medieval masterpiece which has come to symbolize Florence as much as its other architectural gems.

Many other bridges around the world have become instantly recognizable constructions. Sydney Harbour Bridge in Australia, which opened in 1932, has grown to symbolize the city of Sydney just as Brooklyn Bridge across the East River has come to represent New York. In London, to the east of London Bridge, stands Tower Bridge, built after an open competition in the mid-1870s, which attracted over 50 design responses. Between 1886–1894, the bridge was constructed using five major contractors and an army of over 400 construction workers. The construction of the bridge's famous towers and the walkways between them was supported by two immense piers that were sunk into the river bed. The framework for the towers, which rested on the piers, and the walkways employed more than 11,000 tons of steel. The steel framework itself was then protected by covering it in Cornish granite and Portland stone, which also enhanced its appearance. The bridge is not only famous for its towers, but for its central span, which even today splits into two and rises to an angle of 86° to allow river traffic such as tall ships to pass through.

Newton said, 'We build too many walls and not enough bridges.' So let us build more bridges, to connect and delight the world.

Questions 28–34

Complete each sentence with the correct ending, A–I, below.

28 Longer and wider Roman bridges were
29 Darby's bridge was
30 The Zhaozhou Bridge was
31 The rolling bridge was
32 The old London Bridge was
33 The bridge over the Arno in Florence is
34 Numerous bridges around the globe are

> A designed for pedestrians.
> B replaced by a standard arched bridge.
> C rebuilt in a different country.
> D made possible by the use of the arch.
> E covered with shops.
> F constructed as part of a competition.
> G decorated with delicate carvings.
> H made famous by being the first made of iron.
> I considered as iconic landmarks.

Questions 35–40

Complete the flow chart below.

*Choose **ONE WORD OR A NUMBER ONLY** from the passage for each answer.*

The construction of Tower Bridge

Open competition for bridge design – over 50 submissions

↓

Built over eight years by an **35** .... of labourers

↓

Towers built on huge **36** .... with foundations
deep in the **37** .... of the river

↓

On the foundations, a **38** .... made of steel was constructed

↓

This was then encased in two types of stone, protecting the steel and
improving the **39** ....

↓

Central road span with two sections – each going up in the middle to
40 .... degrees

Now check your answers to Reading Passage 3.

Academic Writing 60 minutes

WRITING TASK 1

You should spend about 20 minutes on this task.

> *The charts below show the importance of green space to people in England in 2009 and the volume of visits to the natural environment in 2009–10 and 2010–11.*
>
> *Summarize the information by selecting and reporting the main features, and make comparisons where relevant.*

Write at least 150 words.

Importance of green space to people in England in 2009

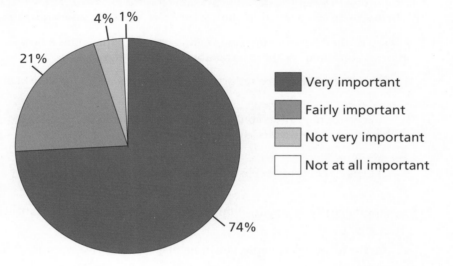

Volume of visits to the natural environment in 2009/10 and 2010/11 in England

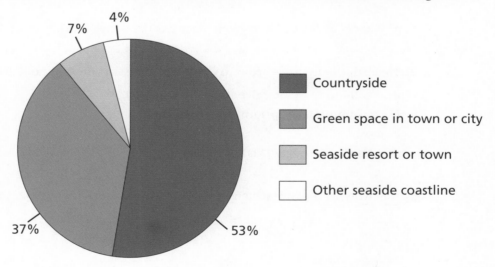

Total – 2.49 billion visits

Before you write your answer to Writing Task 1, go to pages 58–59.

Tips
Writing Task 1

- Read the rubric and think of ways to paraphrase it.
- Write words and phrases (e.g. a large proportion) next to the sections of the charts as you study them.
- Think of a link between the pie charts.
- Make a list of the verbs you need to describe pie charts (e.g. account for) to avoid repetition and show your range of vocabulary.

- Number the information in the order you are going to write about it.
- Think of a possible overview sentence to summarize each chart and also all the data.
- Check the minimum number of words required.

Avoiding repetition

It is important to be able to describe the same information in different ways in Writing Task 1. This helps you to avoid repetition and to increase your vocabulary range and structures.

1 Look at the first pie chart on page 57 and answer the questions below about the information. Then use the information to write full sentences.

  a What was stated as very important by the vast majority of people in England in 2009?

  ....

  b What words or phrases could describe the proportion of people in England that stated that green space was very important?

  ....

  c What percentage of people in England stated green space was very important?

  ....

  d How much did those who thought green space was very important account for?

  ....

  e Was the majority of people who thought green space was very important overwhelming?

  ....

  f How did people rate the importance of green space?

  ....

  g Was people's attitude to green space positive or negative?

  ....

2 Match the items in **a–e** below to words and phrases in the questions above.

  a mention/cite/quote/give as/say (it is/they are)
  b constitute/make up/form/represent/total/comprise
  c most
  d consider (as)/regard (as)
  e value

3 Now write at least three sentences about people who thought green space was *fairly important*.

  ....
  ....
  ....
  ....
  ....
  ....

4 Look at the extract below from a bar graph, which showed factors motivating people to visit the natural environment in 2013. Add the words and phrases in brackets to the correct blank space in sentences **a–e** below.

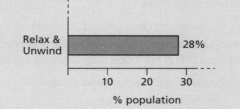

Relax & Unwind 28%

10   20   30

% population

a A sizeable .... of .... (28%) ....
wanting to relax and unwind .... a motivating ....
(*as/respondents/factor/proportion/gave*)

b .... cited wanting to relax and unwind as .... in
.... the natural environment.
(*a factor/twenty-eight per cent/using*)

c .... was stated .... of respondents as a factor
.... the natural environment.
(*for visiting/by 28%/wanting to relax and unwind*)

d Wanting to relax and unwind .... (28%) of
those ....
(*a significant proportion/accounted for/who visited the natural environment*)

e .... (28%) .... wanting to relax and unwind
....
(*as a motivating factor/gave/just over a quarter of respondents*)

5 Look at the second pie chart on page 57 and write sentences using the words below. More than one answer may be possible.

a make/more than half/countryside/53%/visits

....

....

b more than a third/green space in towns and cities/visits/37%/account for

....

....

c seaside resorts or towns/7%/visits/only 4%/compared to/constitute/for other seaside coastline

....

....

6 It is important to make complex sentences by combining information.

a Combine sentences **a** and **b** in Exercise 5 using *compared to*.

b Combine sentences **a** and **b** in Exercise 5 using *although*.

c Expand sentence **c** in Exercise 5 using *while*.

7 Classify the summaries below as relating to pie chart 1, pie chart 2 or the overview for both pie charts.

a More visits are made to the countryside than any other part of the natural environment.   ....

b Overall, green space is valued by the majority of people with visits to green spaces in towns and cities accounting for a sizeable proportion of visits.   ....

c It is clear that green space is of great value to people in England.   ....

Now check your answers to these exercises, and then write your own answer to Writing Task 1. When you have done this, compare what you have written with the possible answers on page 140.

WRITING TASK 2

You should spend about 40 minutes on this task.

Write about the following topic:

> *In many countries, online shopping is becoming more and more popular. Some people think that this is having a negative impact on society.*
>
> *To what extent do you agree or disagree?*

Give reasons for your answer and include any relevant examples from your own knowledge or experience.

Write at least 250 words.

Before you write your answer to Writing Task 2, go to pages 61–62.

Tips
Writing Task 2

- Read the whole rubric for the task carefully.
- Underline key words and check what you are being asked to give your opinion about: *the first sentence only; the second sentence only or the opinion in the second sentence about the first sentence.*
- Make sure you think of ideas and write about both the positive and negative sides or aspects of the argument.
- Think of three main ideas, one for each body paragraph.
- Plan the essay according to paragraphs. Aim for five paragraphs (introduction, three body paragraphs and a conclusion).
- Think of ways to paraphrase the topic in the rubric for your introduction.
- Always check your answer for mistakes.
- Write at least 250 words and divide your answer into clear paragraphs.

Topic analysis

1 Does the first sentence in the Writing Task on page 60 state a situation, a development/ trend or an opinion? Which words indicate this?

....

2 Does the second sentence contain an opinion of one group of people? Which words indicate this?

....

3 Do the words *To what extent do you agree or disagree?* ask you to:
   a write about the increase in popularity of online shopping or
   b respond to a negative view about this increase?

....

Collecting ideas

Collecting ideas about a writing topic can be done in different ways. These techniques can help you respond quickly to any topic.

Technique 1

a It is possible to collect and organize ideas using different perspectives about a topic. Write down ideas that relate to these perspectives: *technological, employment, health, economic/financial, social, age (young/elderly).*

....

....

....

....

....

b What other perspectives can you write about?

....

Technique 2

It is possible to generate ideas using the opposite of another idea. What are the opposite ideas of those you produced in Technique 1a?

....

....

....

....

....

....

Technique 3

It is possible to generate ideas by listing words associated with a topic and then using the words to generate ideas. List five words you associate with online shopping and then think of an idea for each word.

....

....

....

....

....

Planning your essay

A basic essay plan consists of five paragraphs: *introduction, three body paragraphs* and a *conclusion*. It is useful to begin each body paragraph with a statement which summarizes the content of the paragraph (i.e. a topic sentence).

Are the following topic sentences suitable for Writing Task 2 on page 60?

1 It is understandable that some people feel online shopping is detrimental to society, because it is destroying town centres and people's jobs.

2 I personally feel that shopping online has an important role to play in modern life.

3 Another reason why shopping online is beneficial is the freedom it gives to people to do shopping at any time.

Now check your answers to these exercises, and then write your own answer to Writing Task 2. When you have done this, compare what you have written with the possible answers on pages 140–141.

Speaking 11–14 minutes

PART 1 INTRODUCTION AND INTERVIEW (4–5 MINUTES)

In this part, the examiner will check your identification and you will introduce yourself. He/She will ask you about yourself, your home, work or studies and other familiar topics.

Example

Rooms

- Do you have a favourite room in your home? [Why/Why not?]
- What kind of furniture or equipment is there in your favourite room? [Why?]
- Do you think it is better to share a room or have your own room? [Why?]
- Why do you think accommodation in towns and cities has fewer rooms than in the countryside?

PART 2 TASK CARD (3–4 MINUTES)

> **Describe a place you have been to where you listened to some music.**
>
> **You should say:**
> **where the place is**
> **when you went there**
> **who you went with**
> **and explain why you went to this place.**

You will have to talk about the topic for one to two minutes.
You have one minute to think about what you are going to say.
You can make some notes to help you if you wish.

Before you practise the task, go to the Further Practice and Guidance section on page 64.

PART 3 DISCUSSION (4–5 MINUTES)

Discussion topics:

Learning music

Example questions:

- Do you think learning music is more popular now than it was in the past? Why/Why not?
- Should everyone learn to play a musical instrument or sing? Why/Why not?
- Some people think that music should be taught in primary and secondary schools. To what extent do you agree or disagree?

The commercialization of music

Example questions:

- How does modern technology help musicians to be commercially successful? (e.g. the internet, electronic devices)
- Does the media have a positive or negative influence on the music young people buy? Why?
- Some people say that the music industry is only interested in making money nowadays and not in producing quality music. Do you agree?

Before you practise the task, go to the Further Practice and Guidance section on page 65.

Part 2: Task card

In Speaking Part 2, you need to be able to speak naturally in an organized way and without too much hesitation about a topic on a task card. It is important to make short notes and to glance at them briefly as you speak. Build a bank of phrases that you can use again and again.

Look at the Part 2 task card on page 63 and the extract below from a talk about the card. Match the phrases **a–i** below to phrases in the extract. Use each phrase once only.

a The place I'd like to talk about is

....

b during my first year

....

c once a month

....

d Many things made me go there for the first time

....

e I imagine it was probably because

....

f it was a chance to

....

g so that's what appealed to me about

....

h it was definitely worth it

....

i it was a really useful thing to do

....

I'm going to describe a place that I went to for the first time with a friend when I was in my first year of university. It was a folk music club, which was run by students. The club was held monthly in the university student common room. There are many reasons why I first went there, but I think it was mainly because it gave me an opportunity to meet friends and to listen to music that I liked. I didn't know much about folk music and I hadn't heard many live musicians or singers, so that also attracted me to the club. At each event, there was a different group or singer who was fairly well known. We had to pay a small entrance fee to help pay for the performers, but it wasn't very much and it was always worthwhile. The club was also a place where I could listen to music that I hadn't heard before or didn't know much about, so in that sense it was a very valuable experience.

Now check your answers to this exercise.

Make brief notes about a place where you have been to listen to music and then talk about the Part 2 task card on page 63.

Tips

Part 3: Discussion

- Try not to repeat the words used by the examiner. If possible, paraphrase what the examiner says.
- Try to avoid hesitating and try to avoid using unnecessary fillers at the beginning of your answer.
- Learn to begin well as this will give you confidence to develop your answer.

- Develop your answer using reasons and examples. Think of a context for the answers, e.g. your home country. This will help you provide answers.
- Speak fluently at natural speed, but not fast.
- Be sensitive to turn-taking, especially as you know that the examiner will be asking you a series of questions.

Ways to begin

When you answer questions, it is important that you begin well and that you don't hesitate. Hesitation is not just about silence, but also about delaying the answer by putting in unnecessary words and phrases. Your answer needs to match the question. So practise beginning, and then developing your answers.

1 Look at the sentences and phrases below and the first set of questions on *Learning music* on page 63. Choose two alternatives which you can use to begin the answer to each of the three questions.

1

a *Learning music is very popular nowadays.*

b *I think so, because there're more opportunities for young people.*

c *Yes, in my opinion it is, because there're more opportunities for young people.*

2

a *I suppose mainly because it's not just enjoyable but also relaxing.*

b *I think it depends on the person. In my case, for example, …*

c *I believe that playing a musical instrument or singing are important, so yes.*

3

a *From my own point of view, I'd say yes, it ought to be.*

b *Whether music should be taught in all primary and secondary schools is a debatable issue and there are many arguments …*

c *There are many views about this, but to me …*

---

2 Which words or phrases in Exercise 1 above indicate the speaker's opinion? What other ways do you know to express opinion?

....

....

....

....

Now check your answers and practise asking and answering the questions in Part 3 on page 63.

Test 3

Listening approximately 30 minutes

SECTION 1 *Questions 1–10* 🎧 2.1–2.6

Questions 1–6

Choose the correct letter, A, B or C.

Arranging storage

Example

Marina wants to move out

(A) all her belongings.
B some of her belongings.
C all her CDs.

---

1 Marina wants to store

    A books and a wardrobe.
    B books and clothes.
    C books and pictures.

2 The landlord owns

    A all of the furniture.
    B some of the furniture.
    C none of the furniture.

3 What will Marina do with her fragile items?

    A pack them
    B put them into storage
    C take them home

4 How much, in total, will the storage cost?

    A £15 per week, boxes included
    B £15 per week, plus £1 for the boxes
    C £15 per week, plus £15 for the boxes

5 What will happen to the filled boxes to prevent loss?

    A They will be wrapped separately in plastic.
    B They will be stored along with the furniture.
    C They will each be given a unique reference number.

6 Marina would like her things picked up on

    A Thursday morning.
    B Monday morning.
    C Thursday afternoon.

Questions 7–10

Complete the form below.

*Write **NO MORE THAN ONE WORD AND/OR A NUMBER** for each answer.*

CUSTOMER DETAILS	
Name:	Marina **7** ....
Collection address:	37, Turnpike Road, Vale
Postcode:	**8** ....
Box delivery date:	**9** ....
Box collection date:	24th June
Payment type:	online
Booking reference:	**10** ....

Stop the recording when you hear 'That is the end of Section 1.'

Now check your answers to Section 1 of the test.

SECTION 2 *Questions 11–20* 🎧 2.7–2.11

Questions 11–13

Complete the sentences below.

Write ONE WORD ONLY for each answer.

The Hope Centre

11 The new centre opened in ....

12 The original plan was to renovate the building by .... indoors and outside.

13 After the Annual General Meeting, the centre employed an ....

Questions 14–16

Choose THREE letters, A–G.

Which THREE facilities at the centre are new?

A an information centre

B a vending machine

C a sports hall

D a computer suite

E a dance studio

F a stationery shop

G a training room

Questions 17–20

Complete the table below.

Write NO MORE THAN TWO WORDS for each answer.

Staff at the centre

Name	Post	Duties
Akbar Iqbal	Youth Worker	In charge of youth activities and 17 ....
Maria Tuff	Centre Manager	The 18 .... of the centre
Martin Webb	19 .... Coordinator	In charge of a 20 .... of 10 people

Stop the recording when you hear 'That is the end of Section 2.'

Before you check your answers to Section 2 of the test, go to pages 69–70.

Tips

Questions 11–13 and 17–20: Predicting answers

- Always keep in mind the context of the section. This is given at the beginning of the recording, in titles for the whole page, in titles for tables and in the questions.
- Skim the set of questions mentioned at the beginning of the recording. The time allocated to do this varies from 30–40 seconds.
- Think of the possible answers from the point of view of grammar.

- Predict possible answers, even if they may be wrong.
- Underline or circle key words in sentences and tables.
- Keep in mind the headings in tables.
- Be aware of the structures used in each column of tables. It is easy to forget this as you read across a table.
- Make sure the spelling of your answers is correct.
- Make sure you stick to the word limit and do not add words that are already in the questions.

It is important that you develop the skill of predicting the content of gaps in tables, sentences and notes in terms of:

a the grammatical content.

b the vocabulary based on the context.

Look at Questions 11–13 on page 68, and predict:

a the grammar of the missing word.

b possible answers based on the context.

Question 11

a ....   b ....

Question 12

a ....   b ....

Question 13

a ....   b ....

Now do the same for the gaps in the table, Questions 17–20 on page 68.

Question 17

a ....   b ....

Question 18

a ....   b ....

Question 19

a ....   b ....

Question 20

a ....   b ....

Tips

Questions 14–16: Selecting items

- Keep the context in mind.
- Predict possible answers.
- Avoid underlining too many words or phrases.

- Keep in mind that the items are not usually in the order they are mentioned.
- Remember the answers can be written in any order on the answer sheet.

Some questions require you to select items from a list. There will be more items than you need and some of the items might be mentioned in the Listening, but may not be part of the answer. Some items might not be mentioned at all.

Look at the rubric for Questions 14–16, and decide which of the following is the key word.

a facilities **b** centre **c** new

Now check your answers to these tasks. When you have done so, listen to Section 2 again and decide whether you wish to change any of your original answers. Then check your answers to Section 2 of the test.

SECTION 3 Questions 21–30 🎧 2.12–2.16

Questions 21–24

Choose the correct letter, A, B or C.

Work placement

21 Erica's bank's policy document says its employees are

    A committed to helping the environment.

    B an essential part of the business.

    C focused on building their careers.

22 Erica says that workers are

    A invited to get involved in how the business functions.

    B encouraged to keep as fit and as active as possible.

    C advised to attend workshops to increase motivation.

23 Mark believes that Erica's work placement is

    A useful for making new contacts.

    B a challenging place to work in.

    C an experience she will benefit from.

24   According to Erica, what do the bank's working practices lead to?

    A better qualifications for the graduate employees

    B an increase in monthly profits for the bank

    C genuine advantages for customers and clients

Questions 25–30

Complete the flow chart below.

*Write **NO MORE THAN TWO WORDS** for each answer.*

EMPLOYEE ASSESSMENT AND APPRAISAL SYSTEM

DAILY

– Open door policy – talk to senior staff

– Regular internal emails – info about updates to

25 .... and ....

↓

WEEKLY

– Team meetings – share info and ideas

– Good chance to exchange 26 ....

↓

MONTHLY

– Motivational meetings – personal involvement encouraged

THREE-MONTHLY

– Informal interview with 27 .... to discuss staff progress and objectives

– Focus on improving 28 .... and progression opportunities

↓

YEARLY

– Bonus scheme – 29 .... and extra days off for top achievers

---

↓

BIANNUALLY

– Official appraisal system – detailed look at everyone's

30 .... and ....

Stop the recording when you hear 'That is the end of Section 3.'

Before you check your answers to Section 3 of the test, go to page 73.

Tips

Questions 25–30: Completing a flow chart

- Make sure you skim the flow chart before you listen.
- Listen for key words in the notes and any headings.
- Keep listening as you write your answers and make sure you do not lose concentration.
- Note the nature of the information in the questions: notes, semi-notes, clauses or sentences, as this affects the answer.

- As you practise for the IELTS test, learn to process the notes very quickly so that you understand the relationships between the words and phrases.
- Make sure your spelling on the answer sheet is correct and you do not exceed the word limit.
- Do not put words from the questions on the answer sheet.

In this type of completion exercise, it is important that you are ready for the answer as there is a lot of information to read.

Answer the following questions about the flow chart on page 72.

1 What is the purpose of the overall heading?

....

2 What is the purpose of the headings in bold?

....

3 What is the purpose of this kind of listening task?

....

4 Is the text in note form or sentences?

....

5 Is it useful to expand the notes quickly as you read?

....

6 Is it possible to predict the answers of some blanks? How?

....

Now check your answers to this task. When you have done so, listen to Section 3 again and decide whether you wish to change any of your original answers. Then check your answers to Section 3 of the test.

SECTION 4 *Questions 31–40* 🎧 2.17–2.19

Questions 31–34

Choose the correct letter, A, B or C.

31 The initial emphasis of responsible tourism was on
   A places and people on the planet.
   B the effects of inaction.
   C the physical environment.

32 In Tanzania, the local Maasai people
   A are given all of the profits.
   B help make decisions.
   C focus on tourism in game reserves.

33 In Indonesia, the areas for diving and fishing are
   A just next to each other.
   B completely separate from each other.
   C beneficial to the tour operators.

34 To help preserve the heritage of a country, visitors should
   A avoid leaving their holiday complex.
   B have enjoyable experiences.
   C connect with local people.

Questions 35–40

Complete the notes below.

*Write **NO MORE THAN TWO WORDS** for each answer.*

How to be a Responsible Tourist

Before departure

– Do some research into destination by looking at **35** ....

  and guidebooks

– Learn some of the language

– Appropriate **36** .... required

At the destination

– Friendliness and participation required

– Better to use local shops – no purchases of **37** ....

– Use of local guides and public transport

– Avoidance of purchases made from **38** .... – encouragement

  of illegal traders

– No disturbance of archaeological sites

On return

– For the tour operators, comments about enjoyment and potential

  39 .... are beneficial

– Participation in **40** .... and sharing of experiences

Stop the recording when you hear 'That is the end of Section 4.'

Now check your answers to Section 4 of the test.

Academic Reading 60 minutes

READING PASSAGE 1

*You should spend about 20 minutes on **Questions 1–13**, which are based on Reading
Passage 1 below.*

Understanding the links between climate change and development

DEVELOPMENT GOALS around the world are threatened by climate change, with the greatest impact on poor countries and poor people. Climate change cannot be controlled unless growth in all countries produces fewer greenhouse gases. Action needs to be taken now before countries' decisions about development lock the world into increased carbon production and future warming. A lack of change could lead to temperature increases of 5°C or more this century. And we must act together: postponing any reduction of the problem in developing countries could double costs, which could well happen unless substantial financing is used. But if we act now and act together, the costs of keeping warming to around 2°C are modest and can be justified.

In about 2200 BC, a shift in the Mediterranean westerly winds and a reduction in the Indian monsoon produced 300 years of lower rainfall and colder temperatures that hit agriculture from the Aegean Sea to the Indus River. This change in climate brought down Egypt's pyramid-building Old Kingdom and Sargon the Great's empire in Mesopotamia. After only a few decades of lower rainfall, cities along the northern Euphrates were deserted and fell into ruins.

Even intensively irrigated southern Mesopotamia, with its sophisticated bureaucracy and elaborate rationing, could not react fast enough to the new conditions. Without the shipments of rain-fed grain from the north, and faced with dry irrigation ditches and migrants from the devastated northern cities, the empire collapsed.

Societies have always depended on the climate, but are only now beginning to understand that the climate depends on their actions. The steep increase in greenhouse gases since the Industrial Revolution has transformed the relationship between people and the environment. In other words, not only does climate affect development, but development affects the climate.

Left unmanaged, climate change will undo development progress and affect the well-being of current and future generations. It is certain that the Earth will become warmer on average, at extraordinary speed. The effects will be felt everywhere, but much of the damage will be in developing countries. Millions of people from Asian countries such as Bangladesh will suffer as the sea level rises, inundating settlements and contaminating fresh water. Greater rainfall variability and more severe droughts in semi-arid Africa will hinder efforts to enhance food security and combat malnourishment. The hastening disappearance of the glaciers such as the Andean glaciers in South America – which regulate river flow, generate hydropower and supply clean water for millions of people on farms and in cities – will threaten rural incomes and major food markets.

That is why decisive, immediate action is needed. Even though the debate about the costs and benefits of lessening climate change continues, the case is very strong for immediate action to avoid unmanageable increases in temperature. The unacceptable and potentially catastrophic effects that are irreversible and the uncertainty about how, and how soon, they could occur require bold actions. The lack of action in the climate system, in the built environment, and in the behaviour of individuals and institutions means that this action is urgent and immediate.

Over the past two centuries, the direct benefits of carbon-intensive development have been concentrated largely in today's high-income countries. The imbalance in the global distribution of past and current emissions, and in current and future damages, is clear. But if countries are willing to act, there are clear economic incentives for a global deal.

The window of opportunity to choose the right policies to deal with climate change and promote development is closing. The further countries continue to produce emissions at the current rate, the harder it will be to change course and alter infrastructures, economies and lifestyles. High-income countries must face the task of cutting their own emissions by reshaping their built and economic environments. They also need to promote and finance the move to low-carbon growth in developing countries. Improvements in existing practices and basic changes – in the management of natural resources, energy provision, urbanization, social safety nets, international financial transfers, technological innovation – are needed to meet the challenge.

Increasing people's opportunities and material well-being without undermining the sustainability of development is still the main challenge for large parts of the world. Making sure that financial markets around the world are stable and protecting the economy, labour markets and vulnerable groups are immediate priorities. But the world must exploit this moment of opportunity for international cooperation and domestic intervention to tackle the rest of development's problems. Among them, and a top priority, is climate change.

Questions 1–3

*Choose the correct letter, **A, B, C** or **D**.*

1 Climate change can be controlled if countries

   A reduce their growth rates.
   B make new development decisions.
   C focus only on reducing carbon production.
   D take joint action.

2 The shift in the Mediterranean winds around 2200 BC led to

   A a drier and colder world.
   B the destruction of early pyramids.
   C the development of desert cities.
   D increased prosperity along the Euphrates.

3 Which of these contributed to the collapse of the Mesopotamian Empire?

   A intensive irrigation systems
   B the elaborate forms of rationing
   C the end of grain shipments
   D a reduction in migrant workers

Questions 4–7

Classify the following as possible impacts of unmanaged climate change relating to

   A Asia
   B South America
   C Africa

4 The fight against hunger will be held back.

5 Glaciers will disappear quickly.

6 The homes of many people will be flooded.

7 People's livelihoods will be affected.

Questions 8–12

Complete the summary using the list of words, A–J, below.

Immediate action on climate change

It is obvious that immediate action is needed to deal with climate change and thus avoid rises in temperature, the **8** .... of which could be disastrous and impossible to reverse. In the past, wealthy nations gained from carbon-intensive development, but they must now reduce their **9** .... and simultaneously assist developing countries with non carbon-intensive **10** .... It is vital that development is sustainable, but also that people are given more **11** .... and their material well-being is safeguarded. Climate change is only one of the many **12** .... associated with development, but the opportunity to deal with such concerns – through a combination of domestic intervention and international cooperation – should not be ignored.

A challenge	**B** emissions	**C** causes
D priorities	**E** consequences	**F** advances
G chances	**H** benefits	**I** difficulties
J finance		

Question 13

*Choose the correct letter, **A, B, C** or **D**.*

13 What is the writer's overall purpose of writing this article?

    A to compare the situation in past civilizations with the present
    B to show that climate change is inevitable
    C to argue for more action to prevent climate change
    D to reassure people about the future of development

Before you check your answers to Reading Passage 1, go to page 80.

Tips

Questions 4–7: Classification

- Look carefully at the rubric and underline or circle key words.
- Locate the classifying items such as periods of time or places that you are going to use to classify information. These will be in the order in which they first appear in the text.
- Note that these items may be repeated several times and they may be in one or more paragraphs.

- Put a box or circle around the classifying items in the reading passage. This will help you focus your attention.
- Skim the information to be classified. It may be presented in phrases or sentences.
- Look for key words and phrases.
- Match the information to the classifying items. Note you do not have to do these in any particular order.

Classification is a useful way of organizing information in a text. To help you focus on the information, put a box around the words and phrases in the text that you use to classify, e.g. the three continents in the reading passage.

1 Classify the following statements and phrases according to the time frames in **A** and **B**. Put a box around the relevant word/phrases in the reading passage. Remember that there may be paraphrases.

   1 Agriculture was affected.
   2 An empire came to an end.
   3 The level of greenhouse gases changed.
   4 There was a change in wind direction.
   5 Temperatures dropped.

A the Industrial Revolution
B early history

2 Classify the information below according to the locations in **A**, **B** and **C**.

   1 Villages will suffer from floods.
   2 People depart from urban areas.
   3 People in rural areas will lose their jobs.
   4 Drinking water will become unsafe to drink.

A Egypt
B Bangladesh
C South America

3 Classify the information below according to possible future causes in **A**, **B** and **C**.

   1 difficulty in fighting starvation
   2 the difficulty of growing crops
   3 a lack of food to sell
   4 an impact on rivers
   5 the need to migrate

A Wind change and Indian monsoon
B Changes in rain patterns
C The disappearance of glaciers

Question 13: Global multiple-choice question

There are various techniques you can use to help you answer multiple-choice questions that relate to the purpose or the title of the passage. Decide which six of the following suggestions are useful.

a Don't read the question at the beginning so you can think about it while answering other questions.

b Read the whole passage again.

c Look at the title, introduction and conclusion quickly.

d Answer the global multiple-choice question first.

e Answer the global multiple-choice question last.

f Don't think about the purpose or title first before you read the alternatives.

g Skim the other questions quickly.

h Answer by excluding some of the alternatives.

i Read several paragraphs at random.

     Now check your answers to these exercises. When you have done so, decide whether you wish to change any of your answers to Reading Passage 1. Then check your answers to Reading Passage 1 in the Key.

READING PASSAGE 2

*You should spend about 20 minutes on **Questions 14–26**, which are based on Reading
Passage 2 below.*

3D Printing
– the future is already here

The technology behind 3D printers has been around for years, but it is only fairly
recently that 3D printing has started to affect the way the world views production and
manufacturing. Its origins can be found in making prototypes for aerospace and, later,
for automotive companies, and more recently for surgeons who need to make exact
replacements for bones. Usage is now expanding and 3D printers are creating a huge
variety of objects from jewellery to kitchen utensils.

But the main question is how big is 3D printing going to become? Estimates vary, but
Terry Wohlers, an analyst who has followed the field for years, argues that the
technology is about to expand into wider usage that we will see every day. And Pete
Basiliere, Research Director at the analysts Gartner, has said: 'many people think
the technology is some years away, when it is available now and is affordable to
most organizations.'

So how does 3D printing work? Designing objects on a computer is the first step.
This digital blueprint is then used to build a three-dimensional object by adding
numerous super-thin layers to create intricate finished objects. Jonathan Rowley,
Design Director at Digits2Widgets – one of the companies at the forefront of this
new technology, takes the frame of a pair of glasses out of a basin of white powder.
Made of plastic, they are the same white as the powder, but hard. 'We made these
here,' Rowley says, 'The thing is, you couldn't make them any other way.' He points
to the tiny detail at each segment on the hinge, and how creating it in the closed
position means the plastic arms try to stay closed – so the design is at its strongest
when open, yet clings to your head. But, most importantly, it's also a single piece.
This means that no assembly is required, apart from adding lenses.

Inside an oven, a 30 cm-deep basin of powder is heated to just below the powder's
melting point. Heat is then applied by a laser 3,000 times to predefined points over a
layer just 0.1 mm deep, melting and fusing the powder. The end product is a solid
object surrounded by powder. When the powder is washed off, the finished product
emerges. The frames Rowley has created will, after high-pressure cleaning and
colouring, become designer sunglasses, selling for about £425. They only cost £36
to make – but a £150,000 3D printing machine is needed to produce them.

The bigger question is whether everyone will own a 3D printer to use at home or whether such machines will remain a technique that stays in specialist high street shops. In future, if the knob on a washing machine breaks, will people download a file and 'print out' a new one? And what is the limit to what can be made? Like many web-based developments, 3D printing is something that is very difficult for governments to monitor and control effectively.

Olaf Diegel, a professor of mechatronics at Massey University in New Zealand, thinks that 'Probably in the near future we will see people going to a specialist shop and having products printed. Another ten years after that, I believe that we will start to see home ownership appearing, as the quality of the machines improves, prices come down and, mainly, ease of use (particularly of the 3D design software) improves.'

Some think developments could go further. James McBennett, co-founder of fabsie.com, thinks that the power of 3D printing lies in making the computer files that control 3D printers available to everyone, so they can make objects locally. McBennett thinks the really interesting path is the digitization of information about the manufacture of products. 'Say with furniture – at the moment you can only get desks in particular sizes. If you want a desk that, say, can also double as a doghouse, where do you go? With this, designers could write the file, you download it and get it made. The possibilities are endless.'

Dan Crow, who has created a perfect scale model of a famous railway engine, says, 'The really interesting thing is that we're moving away from mass production. First, we had the Industrial Revolution, which was about economies of scale. Then we had the Digital Revolution with the internet. Now we're having the Digitization Revolution, where you can create one or 100s of anything in incredibly high quality.' One major advantage of 3D printers is that it doesn't matter if one or one thousand items are produced, the cost of production per item stays constant.

But Rowley is dismissive of the idea that home 3D printing will ever really take off. 'I'm unsure about the general public's urge to create things,' he says, 'People want brands, not to be unique.' In the end, 3D printing is unlikely to ever completely replace traditional manufacturing methods; it is much more likely to complement rather than compete with such methods.

Glossary: *digitization*: changing information into a digital form

Questions 14–18

Look at the following statements (Questions 14-18) and the list of people below.

*Match each statement with the correct person, **A, B, C, D** or **E**.*

14 He believes that access to design data will expand the use of 3D printing.

15 He realizes that a common belief about 3D printing is untrue.

16 He predicts that 3D printing will become more common in the home.

17 He does not believe domestic 3D printing will become widespread.

18 He sees 3D printing as part of an historical process.

List of People

A Pete Basiliere
B Jonathan Rowley
C Olaf Diegel
D James McBennett
E Dan Crow

Questions 19–22

Complete the diagram below.

*Choose **ONE WORD ONLY** from the passage for each answer.*

Printing 3D sunglasses

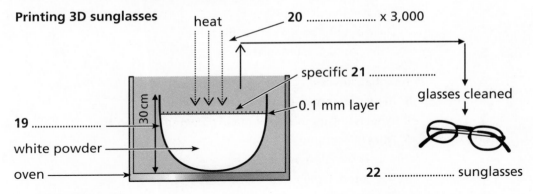

heat

20 .... x 3,000

specific **21** ....

0.1 mm layer

glasses cleaned

19 ....

30 cm

white powder

oven

22 .... sunglasses

Questions 23–26

Answer the questions below.

*Choose **NO MORE THAN THREE WORDS** from the passage for each answer.*

23 From what sector did 3D printing begin?

24 What is the unique feature of the glasses that Rowley makes?

25 What area, exemplified by 3D printing, do governments find hard to monitor and control?

26 In the future, what is the 3D printing industry likely to complement?

Before you check your answers to Reading Passage 2, go to pages 84–85.

Tips

Questions 14–18: Matching statements to people

- Look carefully at the rubric. Check if any of the names can be used more than once and whether there is an item at the end of the list of names which says 'None of the above'.

- Read through the list of names. Note they are in the order they first appear in the text.

- Skim the statements that you need to match. These are not in the order they appear in the text.

- Put a box or a circle around the names in the text. This will help you focus on the information related to the names.

- Note the names may be repeated several times and they may occur throughout the reading passage.

- Be aware that the information in the statements for matching is likely to paraphrase the information in the text.

The questions below and on page 85 will help you to make sure that you have chosen the correct answers for Questions 14–18.

1 Answer the following questions about each person.

A Pete Basiliere

  1 Where in the text is Basiliere mentioned?

  2 Does he mention

    a access to design data?

    b a common belief?

    c home 3D printing?

    d any reference to history?

  3 Does he talk about what people think?

  4 Is the popular belief correct?

B Jonathan Rowley

  1 In how many paragraphs is Rowley mentioned?

  2 What is Rowley talking about in paragraphs 3 and 4?

  3 Does he mention

    a access to design data?

    b a common belief?

    c home 3D printing?

    d any reference to history?

  4 In paragraph 9, does he mention home 3D printing?

  5 What does he think about the future of home 3D printing?

C Olaf Diegel

  1 Where in the text is Diegel mentioned?

  2 Does he mention

    a access to design data?

    b a common belief?

    c home 3D printing?

    d any reference to history?

  3 Does he talk about the past, present or future of 3D printing?

  4 What does he think about the future of home 3D printing?

D James McBennett

  1 Where in the text is McBennett mentioned?

  2 Does he mention

    a access to design data?

    b a common belief?

    c home 3D printing?

    d any reference to history?

  3 Under what circumstances does he say 3D printing could do even more?

E Dan Crow

  1 Where in the text is Crow mentioned?

  2 Does he mention

    a access to design data?

    b a common belief?

    c home 3D printing?

    d any reference to history?

  3 What does he think 3D printing is a part of?

Each of the statements in Questions 14–18 contains a reference to a person and 3D printing. In this type of question, it is therefore important to recognize the key words in the statement.

2 Look at Questions 14–18 and underline the words in each statement that will help you match it to a person.

Now check your answers to these exercises. When you have done so, decide whether you wish to change any of your answers to Questions 14–18. Then check your answers to Reading Passage 2 in the Key.

READING PASSAGE 3

*You should spend about 20 minutes on **Questions 27–40**, which are based on Reading Passage 3 on the following pages.*

Questions 27–32

Reading Passage 3 has six paragraphs, **A–F**.

*Choose the correct heading for paragraphs **A–F** from the list of headings below.*

List of Headings

  i   Steps taken to create a tea-growing estate

 ii   The origins of Tregothnan Estate

iii   Plans for future expansion

 iv   A scheme for an International Tea Centre

  v   Common misconceptions about growing tea

 vi   The harvest of the first commercial crop of tea

vii   The range of activities the project involves

viii Britain: a surprising island

 ix   A natural environment for growing tea leaves that appeal

---

27 Paragraph **A**

28 Paragraph **B**

29 Paragraph **C**

30 Paragraph **D**

31 Paragraph **E**

32 Paragraph **F**

BRITAIN GROWS ITS OWN TEA

Tregothnan Estate, in England's south-western county of Cornwall, is producing the first tea ever to be grown in British soil.

A Some will be surprised to learn that the tea that is now being grown and manufactured at the Tregothnan Estate, is the first tea ever to be produced in Britain. Others may think that tea has always been grown in Britain, and may therefore wonder what the fuss is all about. There are comments that are not unknown, such as: 'I always buy Yorkshire tea. It's so good to think of it growing out there on the moors,' and 'I only ever buy good old British tea.' However, these are totally misguided. There may be a few ornamental tea bushes dotted around certain British gardens, but they have never been plucked, nor added to the supply of tea that is consumed as the 'national beverage'. In general, the British climate is not kind to the Camellia sinensis plant, making it hard to keep them alive in normal conditions. However, the climate of Cornwall is not so different from that of Darjeeling.

B Since 1335, the Tregothnan Estate, which stands just outside Truro, has belonged to the Boscawen family. Of all the large estates in Cornwall, including Prince Charles's Duchy of Cornwall, this is the largest. Once the decision to grow tea at Tregothnan was taken, samples were collected from the well-known tea bushes growing outdoors in British soil. Next, a camellia fact-finding tour of China, India, Sri Lanka, Korea, Japan and other tea-growing regions of the world was undertaken, to examine camellias for their foliage, flowers, fruit and tea. By 1999, 20 acres of valley (where once potatoes, carrots and peas grew) had been cleared, and the first plantings were made using cutting material and some seeds that were imported from various tea regions. There are now some 30 different clones in the collection of bushes – some of known origin, some unknown and others wild. Advice and help were sought from experts within the industry.

C In spring 2005, the plants were mature enough for the first commercial crop to be plucked. On 3rd May, estate workers became Britain's first ever tea pickers. After withering, rolling, oxidation and drying, approximately 50 kilos of Britain's pioneering, *Single Estate* tea went on sale at one of London's most prestigious stores, Fortnum & Mason in Piccadilly, at the amazing price of £28 for 50 grams, while the blended *Classic* black tea sold for approximately £10 for 50 grams.

D The leaves on the Tregothnan's tea bushes may be free from all the insects and pests that cause problems on estates around the world, but rabbits, deer and pheasants appear to love the tender new leaf buds. There is no action taken against these creatures, which obviously know a good thing when they taste it, since once the bushes reach a certain age, they are more resistant to these animals. The estate may not be registered organic, but the cultivation methods are, and there are plans to be listed as such in the future. On a good day, about 20 kilos of leaf is plucked. However, more time needs to be spent analysing the bushes that give the best leaf, and how variations in manufacturing methods affect the quality and flavour.

E The first five years of the project have been a time of experimentation and testing of bush yield and quality, as well as developing manufacturing methods. Product design, brand image, marketing methods and distribution have also been addressed and planned for. Alongside the business of manufacturing and selling loose leaf tea and tea bags, Tregothnan also sells baby tea bushes to nurseries and private individuals.

F A new area of ground has now been cleared, ready for the next phase of tea planting. The short-term plan is to produce no more, nor any less, than a ton of tea per year. The long-term plan, however, is to develop business slowly, with the focus on quality and sustainability, and still be a successful private operation within a time frame of 15 years. In order to provide a venue that informs and teaches about tea, there are plans to build – on the estates – an International Tea Centre. There will also be a tea factory, in which visitors can see how the tea is actually processed and packed. There will be facilities available for training events, seminars, perhaps exhibitions, conferences, shops and tearooms. 'This is a small beginning, but we feel the opportunity is lost, if all we do is grow tea to sell,' explains a spokesman. 'The tea industry has so much going for it. This is really special, because we have brought together two great British passions – gardening and tea.'

Questions 33–37

Do the following statements agree with the information given in Reading Passage 3?

Write

TRUE	*if the statement agrees with the information*
FALSE	*if the statement contradicts the information*
NOT GIVEN	*if there is no information on this*

33 Nobody believes that tea grows on the Yorkshire moors.

34 The climate of Cornwall is similar to that of Darjeeling.

35 There are estates in Cornwall that are more extensive than Tregothnan.

36 It was not until more than five years after the first planting that the first commercial tea harvest took place.

37 All the tea that went on sale in Fortnum & Mason was sold.

Questions 38–40

Complete the sentences below.

*Choose **NO MORE THAN THREE WORDS** from the passage for each answer.*

38 Tea bushes become .... to pests when they are old enough.

39 If the production methods vary, this can affect the .... of the tea.

40 In addition to making and selling tea, the estate also ....

Now check your answers to Reading Passage 3.

Academic Writing 60 minutes

WRITING TASK 1

You should spend about 20 minutes on this task.

> *The two maps below show changes to Melvin Island between 2000 and 2010.*
>
> *Summarize the information by selecting and reporting the main features, and make comparisons where relevant.*

Write at least 150 words.

Melvin Island in 2000

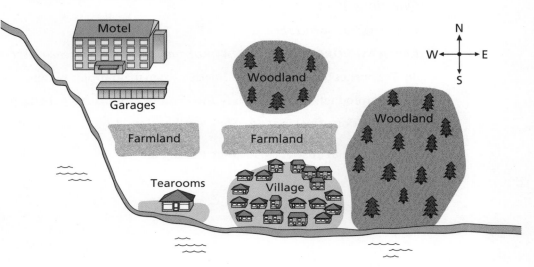

Melvin Island in 2010

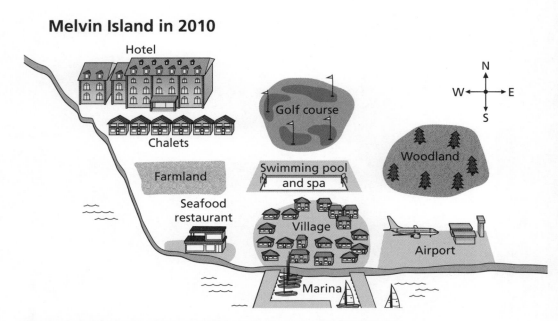

Before you write your answer to Writing Task 1, go to pages 91–92.

Tips

Writing Task 1

- Read the rubric and the task and underline the word 'Summarize'.
- As you look at the maps, number the changes that you want to write about.
- Make notes about the verbs and nouns you want to use.
- Be conscious of the tenses to describe the changes, often the past simple.
- Write the introduction, paraphrasing the rubric as far as you can.

- Make sure you write an overview, as you may not achieve a high score without one.
- Use a wide range of vocabulary and grammar structures including active and passive verbs.
- Check your answer for spelling mistakes.
- Write in paragraphs.
- Make sure you do not write less than 150 words.

Language for describing change in maps: The passive

When describing changes in this kind of task it is often necessary to use the passive. This is because the focus is on *what was done*, i.e. the changes are important, not who carried them out.

1 Put these verbs into the correct column according to their meaning.

renovate	demolish	add	improve	pull down	develop
erect	replace	build	construct	knock down	make way for
extend	turn into	create	modernize	remove	convert into
give way to					

To describe something that is no longer there	To describe something that changed	To describe something that is new

Note that you need to be careful with the collocations of many of these verbs (e.g. *renovate a building*, but not *renovate a tree*). They cannot all be used to describe all of the features.

2 Now use three verbs, one from each column, to describe what happened to the buildings below in a town or city you know. Use the past simple tense, active or passive.

   a A derelict building: ....

   b An old-fashioned hotel: ....

   c A modern leisure centre: ....

Now check your answers to these exercises.

3 Look at the maps in Writing Task 1 and classify the features below according to the three columns in Exercise 1. Some features can appear in more than one column.

| woodland | golf course | motel | swimming pool and spa | farmland |
| airport | marina | garages | tearooms | |

Something that is no longer there	Something that changed	Something that is new

4 It is important to be able to use the points of the compass (north, south, east and west) to say where things are located on maps. You can use other features as landmarks to say where things are: *north of/to the north of, south of/to the south of, east of/to the east of, west of/to the west of.* You can also say *north-east of/to the north-east of,* etc.

Look at the maps again and use the village as a landmark to state where each of the following features are located.

a marina

....

b swimming pool and spa

....

c airport

....

d seafood restaurant

....

e hotel complex

....

Now check your answers to these exercises, and then write your own answer to Writing Task 1. When you have done this, compare what you have written with the possible answers on pages 145–146.

WRITING TASK 2

You should spend about 40 minutes on this task.

Write about the following topic:

> *Life in many cities around the world is becoming so expensive that one day only rich people will be able to live there.*
>
> *What are the causes of this situation? What measures could be taken to solve the problem?*

Give reasons for your answer and include any relevant examples from your own knowledge or experience.

Write at least 250 words.

Before you write your answer to Writing Task 2, go to pages 94–95.

Writing Task 2

Cause and effect relationships

Cause and effect relationships are common in academic writing. They help you to develop ideas, often through a whole paragraph.

Being able to describe cause and effect relationships is necessary in this type of essay. It is also as important in other types of essays as well as in the other three main skills.

1 The lists below contain various causes (**A**) and effects (**B**) relating to life in London. Match each cause to an effect.

A Causes	**B Effects**
i attractiveness as a place to live	a higher chances of finding work
ii large volumes of traffic	b expensive fares
iii demand for public transport	c desire to work there
iv large quantity of people eating out	d high house prices and rents
v crowded tourist attractions	e parking problems
vi many jobs available	f expensive entry fees
vii significantly higher wages	g increase in number of restaurants and cafés

Now check your answers to this exercise.

2 Look at the following verbs, nouns and linking devices which are used to talk about causes [A] and effects [B].

Verbs

	cause	
[A]	*lead to*	[B]
	give rise to	
	result in	
	be caused by	
[B]	*stem from*	[A]
	result from	

Nouns

	be an important factor in	
[A]	*be a significant factor in*	[B]
	have an influence on	
	have an impact on	

An/The effect of [A] *is* [B].
A/The consequence of [A] *is* [B].

Linking devices

[A]. *Therefore,* [B].
[A]. *Because of this,* [B].
[A]. *As a result of this,* [B].
[A]. *Consequently,* [B].

The following sentences have been written from the information in causes (**A**) and effects (**B**) on page 94. Complete the sentences using suitable verbs, nouns or linking devices. Note that there may be more than one possible answer.

a The attractiveness of London as a place to live ....*leads to*............. high house prices and rents.

b There are many jobs available in London. .... , there are higher chances of finding work there.

c Expensive fares in London .... the high demand for public transport.

d The large quantity of people eating out in London .... the increase in the number of restaurants and cafés.

e The large volumes of traffic .... parking problems in London.

f Wages in London are significantly higher than in other cities. .... , a lot of people have a desire to work there.

g .... crowded tourist attractions in London .... expensive entry charges to museums and galleries.

Now check your answers to this exercise.

3 Look again at the topic in Writing Task 2. The statement presents a problem. The first part of the question asks for causes and the second part of the question asks for solutions.

Write down:

two possible causes: ....
....

two possible solutions: ....
....

Now check your answers to this exercise, and then write your own answer to Writing Task 2. When you have done this, compare what you have written with the possible answers on page 146.

Speaking 11–14 minutes

PART 1 INTRODUCTION AND INTERVIEW (4–5 MINUTES)

In this part, the examiner will check your identification and you will introduce yourself. He/She will ask you about yourself, your home, work or studies and other familiar topics.

Example

Tourism

- What places are popular with tourists in your country? [Why?]
- Which tourist places have you enjoyed visiting? [Why/Why not?]
- Do you prefer to visit natural or man-made tourist attractions? [Why?]
- Is there any particular tourist attraction you would like to visit in the future? [Why?]

PART 2 TASK CARD (3–4 MINUTES)

> **Describe an experience that changed your life in a good way.**
>
> **You should say:**
>   **what the experience was**
>   **who you were with**
>   **where and when the experience happened**
> **and explain how the experience changed your life.**

You will have to talk about the topic for one to two minutes.
You have one minute to think about what you are going to say.
You can make some notes to help you if you wish.

Before you practise the task, go to the Further Practice and Guidance section on page 97.

PART 3 DISCUSSION (4–5 MINUTES)

Discussion topics:

Gaining experience

Example questions:

- What are some ways that schoolchildren gain experience of the real world?
- Should all children be made to do work experience while still at school?
- Are there any ways that technology can make it easier for young people to gain experience and skills?

Importance of knowledge and experience

Example questions:

- Which is more important for young people to have nowadays: knowledge or experience? Why?
- In terms of employment, why do some employers value experience over knowledge?
- Do you agree that the knowledge and experience children will need in the future will be the same as today?

Before you practise the task, go to the Further Practice and Guidance section on page 98.

Part 2: Task card

In the test, you will be given paper and a pencil to make notes. It is important you make full use of the minute to write short notes to help you organize your answer.

In this section of the Speaking test, the focus is on describing things such as books, films, gifts, experiences, incidents, events, occasions, people, rules and so on.

Look at the notes you have made for Part 2 on page 96, and use the phrases below to expand your points.

- There have been many important events in my life, but the one I am going to talk about is ....

- It happened when ....

- I was in/at .... at the time.

- It happened because ....

- Since then my life .... ,

  because ....

Now match the question words below to the possible sentence openings. There may be more than one possible answer in each case.

1 Where?   2 When?   3 Who?   4 Why?

a   I was in college as usual ...

    ....

b   It was about a year ago ...

    ....

c   I remember it well, because ...

    ....

d   The reason it was memorable is ...

    ....

e   It happened during my work placement ...

    ....

f   It really stuck in my mind, because ...

    ....

g   It was at a family reunion ...

    ....

h   My family and I were in a museum ...

    ....

i   He was a classmate of mine ...

    ....

Now check your answers to this exercise. Then use the notes above to talk about Speaking Part 2 on page 96.

Part 3: Discussion

Remember that there are no wrong or right answers in this section. Your opinions are not judged; it is your ability to communicate effectively in English that is being assessed.

To prepare to take part in a discussion in this section make notes under the headings below. Note that in the test you cannot make notes for Part 3.

Gaining experience

Work placements and volunteering

....

....

....

What will happen if young people don't gain new knowledge and experience/skills?

....

....

....

Use of technology in training, e.g. online tasks, simulation

....

....

....

Importance of knowledge and experience

Experiences we have of being in a family, class or community

....

....

....

Knowledge gained by studying

....

....

....

Experience needed for the modern world

....

....

....

General experience vs specific skills

....

....

....

Now look at the answers to this exercise. Then answer the questions in Part 3 on page 96 in your own words and using your own examples and experiences.

Test 4

Listening approximately 30 minutes

SECTION 1 *Questions 1–10* 🎧 2.20–2.25

Questions 1–5

Choose the correct letter, A, B or C.

Places to visit

Example

The visitor is

A alone.
Ⓑ with friends.
C with his family.

1 The visitor is more interested in

   A historic London.
   B modern attractions.
   C new buildings.

2 Why does the visitor decide to avoid going to the castle?

   A It is too popular.
   B It is too far away.
   C It is too expensive.

3 The two museums are recommended because they are

   A easy to get to.
   B quite serious.
   C very entertaining.

4 The contemporary art at Tate Modern is largely

   A British.
   B international.
   C European.

5 A private capsule on The London Eye is good if the visitor

   A books a week in advance.
   B has other people to go with.
   C wants a very special treat.

Questions 6–10

Complete the notes below.

Write NO MORE THAN ONE WORD OR A NUMBER for each answer.

General tours

River boat cruises:

– leisurely and **6** .... way to spend the day

– knowledgeable and informative commentaries

Open-top bus tours:

– **7** .... in 10 languages

– can hop on and off

Bicycle tours

– cheaper, small groups

– must be fit

– see **8** .... parts of London

Smartphone apps

– most free

– interactive **9** ....

– app tours available in **10** .... or more languages

Stop the recording when you hear 'That is the end of Section 1.'

Before you check your answers to Section 1 of the test, go to page 101.

Questions 1–5: Multiple-choice questions

In the Listening test, you will often hear points from the multiple-choice options which are, in fact, incorrect. The context of the point in the question *may not be the same* as that in the recording. It is very important that you do not get distracted and think that because you have heard a word or phrase that it must be the correct answer.

The following exercise will help you to focus on choosing the correct multiple-choice option.

Listen again to the first part of Section 1 and answer the following questions.

1 a What does the visitor mostly want to see?

....

   b What does the visitor not want to miss out on?

....

2 a What is popular?

....

   b Does the speaker say something is too popular?

....

   c What is 'quite a way outside London'?

....

3 a Is anything about the location of the museums mentioned?

....

   b Does the visitor want to visit serious museums?

....

   c What does the woman say about the interactive exhibits?

....

4 a What has the man heard about the Tate Modern?

....

   b Is 'international' or a paraphrase of 'international' mentioned?

....

   c Is anything mentioned about British or European art?

....

5 a What two things does the woman say a trip on The London Eye is a chance to do?

....

   b What two conditions does the woman mention about having a private capsule?

....

Now check your answers to this task. When you have done so, listen again to the first part of Section 1 of the test and decide whether you wish to change any of the answers you gave to Questions 1–5. Then check your answers to Section 1 of the test.

SECTION 2 *Questions 11–20* 🎧 2.26–2.30

Questions 11–14

What comments does the speaker make about the following items?

*Choose **FOUR** answers from the box and write the correct letter, **A–F**, next to questions 11–14.*

> A possible to hire
> B necessary to insure
> C owned by school
> D necessary to repair
> E cheap to obtain
> F free of charge

11 a waterproof cover   ....

12 a large tent   ....

13 sound equipment   ....

14 a barbecue   ....

Questions 15–18

Complete the sentences below.

*Write **NO MORE THAN ONE WORD** for each answer.*

Things to organize before the event

15 For safety, an audience-free zone that is .... indicated is essential.

16 The performers will need three hours to set up, and good .... for their vehicles.

17 Near the performance area, a suitable and safety-certificated source of .... is needed.

18 The speaker is sure the .... requirements can be met.

Questions 19 and 20

*Choose the correct letter, **A, B** or **C**.*

19 The performers advertise

    A on the school website.
    B on social media.
    C in local newspapers.

20 The speaker suggests that class teachers should encourage children to

    A offer free tickets for the concert.
    B write an advert for a paper.
    C design posters of the event.

Stop the recording when you hear 'That is the end of Section 2.'

Now check your answers to Section 2 of the test.

SECTION 3 *Questions 21–30* 🎧 2.31–2.35

Questions 21–23

Complete the sentences below.

Write NO MORE THAN TWO WORDS for each answer.

Sophie's article

21 Sophie has chosen an article on .... the funding to certain
    university courses.

22 Sophie's chosen article has made her feel quite ....

23 Sophie thinks that articles like the one she has chosen can affect .... to
    course funding.

Questions 24–27

Complete the table below.

Write ONE WORD ONLY for each answer.

Sophie's comments

Points in article	Contradiction	Reason
more students equipped for modern job market	not everyone suited to studying STEM subjects	difference in people's goals and **24** ....
subjects like art should be self-funded	crucial **25** .... subjects	professionals with different languages needed globally
more university funding for scientists and engineers	enough money is **26** .... into these areas	engineers needed, not at the **27** .... of investment elsewhere

Questions 28–30

Choose THREE letters, A–G.

Which **THREE** points do the speakers mention about organizing a critique?

A   select some main points

B   restate any examples

C   review the contents

D   review minor details

E   write subheadings

F   mention writer's effectiveness

G   comment on writer's clarity

Stop the recording when you hear 'That is the end of Section 3.'

Before you check your answers to Section 3 of the test, go to pages 105–106.

Tips

Listening to dialogues in Section 3

- Work out the context of the dialogue from the instructions at the beginning of the section, the headings and the questions.

- Read the rubrics carefully and predict the answers where possible.

- Note word limits for the questions and be careful with spelling, especially as you transfer your answers to the answer sheet.

- Note the number of speakers from the instructions.

- Be aware that the information for the answers in dialogues may not be given by the speaker named in the questions.

- Be sensitive to the turns taken by the different speakers. One speaker may signal the answer to be given by another.

- Listen for the key words given by all speakers.

- Be aware that there will be a wide range of accents used in the Listening component, but they will be clear.

- Use the time at the end of the section to review your answers. Alternatively, if you are satisfied with your answers, you can go to the questions for the next section.

Questions 21–27

1   For each question below and on page 106, use the positive and negative hints to help you predict the answer for the gaps. Think of word families and synonyms as well as the context. Make notes on the lines below, if necessary. Note that even the opposite of what is required in the blanks can help you predict.

Question 21

an -*ing* form of the verb, something positive, something negative, something related to funding, reducing

....

....

Question 22

an adjective, something to do with emotion, happy, annoyed

....

....

Question 23

two words, a verb, a noun and noun, related to people responsible for funding, something related to views

....

....

Question 24

a noun, plural/singular, something related to 'personal'/a person

....

....

Question 25

a noun, an adverb, something to do with essential, related to curriculum

....

....

Question 26

a past participle, related to water or oil, pour (but stronger)

....

....

Question 27

a singular noun, related to expense, poor

....

....

2   It is often useful when you think about answers to think of word associations or words that belong to the same family. Think of other words which are related to those below.

   a person

     ....

     ....

   b restriction

     ....

     ....

   c choose

     ....

     ....

   d different

     ....

     ....

   e expenditure

     ....

     ....

Now check your answers to these tasks. When you have done so, listen again to the first part of Section 3 of the test and decide whether you wish to change any of the answers you gave to Questions 21–27. Then check your answers to Section 3 of the test.

SECTION 4   *Questions 31–40* 🎧 2.36–2.38

Complete the notes below.

*Write **NO MORE THAN THREE WORDS** for each answer.*

COURSE REVIEW

Work experience

Students benefited from

- work experience before taking the course
- day-release work **31** .... during the course
  - many local companies set up by past students

Qualifications are valued by employers – but also essential to gain **32** .... experience

Diploma graduates – very well **33** .... for job market

Entrepreneurship module

Students to benefit from market trends

- domination by global enterprises
- greater emphasis on small companies, e.g. tech **34** .... – more flexible/agile

Dynamic company with quick reaction to **35** ....

Networking

Students

- had plenty of opportunities to make **36** .... and build up networks
- were shown how systems within organizations work/don't work

'Going it alone'

- shown possible **37** .... faced
- opportunity for future developments

Skills learnt on the course can open up economic potential

- source of new jobs and growth
- benefit the local economy and the **38** .... of the university/department

World skills module

Non-cognitive skills

- opportunity recognition, innovation, **39** .... , resilience, decision-making, etc
- reflection while at work

Finance

Finance sourcing

- setting up independent businesses
- with the university – exciting new **40** .... launched for funding new companies

---

Stop the recording when you hear 'That is the end of Section 4.'

Now check your answers to Section 4 of the test.

Academic Reading 60 minutes

READING PASSAGE 1

*You should spend about 20 minutes on **Questions 1–13**, which are based on Reading Passage 1 below.*

The growth of liquorice

LIQUORICE has a long, honourable history in the service of mankind. Alexander the Great, the Scythian armies and the Roman Emperor Caesar, are all on record for endorsing the beneficial properties contained in liquorice. Warriors used it as a substitute for water on a march, while others recognized liquorice's valuable healing properties.

Native to Asia and the Mediterranean region, liquorice (*Glycyrrhiza glabra*) in the family *Leguminosae* is a tall shrub (1.5 m) with blue or violet flowers. The most common variety, Spanish liquorice, is characterized by blue flowers, while Russian liquorice has violet blossoms. The name *glycyrrhiza* comes from Greek words meaning 'sweet root'. The roots contain the medicinally active constituents, and the plant requires rich soils and grows in subtropical climates. It is indigenous to Turkey, Iraq, Spain, Greece and northern China.

The plants are graceful and their leaves have an almost feathery appearance from a distance. The leaves hang down during the night on each side of the stem, though they do not meet beneath it. From the leaves, spring spikes of small pale-blue, violet or purplish flowers, followed by small pods somewhat resembling a partly-grown pea pod in form.

The underground system, as in so many *Leguminosae*, is double: one part consisting of a vertical or tap root, often with several branches; the other of a horizontal runner, coming off the root below the surface of the ground. These runners have leaf buds and throw up stems in their second year. The perennial downward-running roots, as well as the long horizontal runners, are equally preserved for use.

English-grown liquorice is dug up in late autumn and sold mostly in its fresh state for making extract, with only a small amount being dried. When washed, fresh English liquorice is a bright yellowish brown. It is very flexible, with a light yellow, juicy internal substance, which consists of a thick bark surrounding a woody column. The root has a peculiar earthy odour and a strong, characteristic, sweet taste. The English extract of liquorice, made from the fresh home-grown root, is said to have a more delicate flavour than that of imported varieties.

In southern Italy, large quantities of liquorice root are grown, but it is chiefly converted into extract, though some of the root is exported. Spain and the south of France provide quantities of carefully dried liquorice root. Up to the year 1890, the cultivation of Spanish liquorice was small or moderate in comparison with the wild collection. Owing, however, to the depletion of the natural supplies of good quality root, this cultivation has grown rapidly in southern and southern-central Europe, where the climate is favourable.

Nearly all the Russian liquorice that has been exported has already been peeled. It reaches a much larger size than the Spanish variety, and the taste, although sweet, is accompanied by a subtle bitterness or acridity. It consists chiefly of roots, not runners, in long and often crooked pieces, about 5 cm in thickness. These are pale yellow externally, and are a lighter yellow and softer internally than the Spanish variety.

Spain was formerly the main supplier, which explains why the extract is still referred to as 'Spanish Juice', but the best grade has almost disappeared. The sticks vary in size, but are commonly about 2 cm in diameter and 15 or 18 cm in length. When imported, they are usually wrapped in bay leaves.

Liquorice grows best on sandy soil near streams, and is usually not found in the wild more than 50 metres from water. It will not flourish on clay and prefers the rich, fine soil of lowlands in river valleys, where there is an abundance of moisture during the growing period. Liquorice also flourishes where the ground hardens during the hot, dry summer months.

The plant grows most successfully in a warm climate. Not only can it not endure severe freezing, but cool weather interferes with the formation of the sweet liquorice juice and makes the plant woody. It appears that climates which are particularly favourable for the production of oranges are also favourable for liquorice.

Owing to the depth to which the root penetrates and its propagation the plant is a persistent weed in cultivated grounds, where it is indigenous and exceedingly difficult to remove by its roots. It is very healthy and robust and rarely subject to disease. It can successfully occupy the ground to the exclusion of other plants. For this reason, the continuation of a natural supply may be considered as assured, although it is liable to suffer from severe depletion due to being overpicked.

Questions 1–5

Choose **FIVE** *letters, A–J.*

Which **FIVE** of the following statements about the liquorice plant are true according to the passage?

  A The health properties of liquorice are not well known.
  B Liquorice used to be valued as a means to quench thirst.
  C Liquorice plants only grow in tropical climates.
  D Liquorice blossoms are blue or violet.
  E Liquorice flowers last for a long time.
  F The leaves of the liquorice plant look like feathers.
  G Pods develop on the plant after the flowering stage.
  H Medicine is derived from the flowers of the liquorice plant.
  I The liquorice root system has two roots.
  J Horizontal runners develop stems immediately.

Questions 6–10

Do the following statements agree with the information given in Reading Passage 1?

Write

TRUE   *if the statement agrees with the information*

FALSE   *if the statement contradicts the information*

NOT GIVEN   if there is no information on this

6   Only some of the English liquorice is harvested in the autumn.

7   Imported varieties of liquorice have a stronger taste than English liquorice.

8   After 1890, the production of Spanish liquorice declined slowly.

9   Russian liquorice is not popular because it has a bitter taste.

10   Russian and Spanish varieties of liquorice have identical flavours.

Questions 11–13

Complete each sentence with the correct ending, A–E, below.

11   Wild liquorice is usually found near streams because it

12   To guarantee the development of juice, the liquorice plant

13   In some areas, the liquorice plant is a problem because it

> **A** requires a warm climate.
> **B** flourishes on clay.
> **C** needs a lot of water.
> **D** tolerates very low temperatures.
> **E** spreads very easily.

Before you check your answers to Reading Passage 1, go to page 111.

Tips

Questions 6–10: True/False/Not Given (Comparison and contrast)

- Look at the statements.
- Identify grammar patterns in the statements, e.g. comparison and contrast.
- Think of how comparative adjectives can be paraphrased in the text, e.g. *much smaller than/not as large as.*
- Think of how nouns can be compared and paraphrased, e.g. *more houses than apartments/ fewer apartments than houses.*
- Think of comparison of adverbs, e.g. *more slowly/ not as quickly as.*

- Think of contrast between words of quantity, e.g. *all/the majority of.*
- Check that the items or concepts are compared in the text.
- Make sure you use the statements to analyse the reading passage, and not vice versa.
- Learn to hold the information in the questions in your head as you analyse the reading passage rather than translating as you check the reading passage.
- Build a bank of examples of comparisons and practise paraphrasing them.

In many reading passages and questions, there is a range of terms of comparison and contrast, comparing adjectives (*hotter, more popular, as big as*), nouns (*more people*) and adverbs (*more slowly*). In many question types, these terms will often be paraphrased. It is important to understand which phrases have a similar meaning and which are different.

1 Match the words in **1–5** with the words and phrases in italics from **a–k**.

1 all   ....

....

2 most   ....*the vast majority of*............

....

3 some   ....

....

4 few   ....

....

5 none   ....

....

a *The vast majority of* people disagreed.
b *Not many of* the animals were captured.
c *A number of* cakes were unsold.
d *A small proportion of* items was returned.
e *Not one of* the passengers complained.
f *Without exception* the workers voted for a shorter working day.

g *Each* student was given a welcome pack.
h *Nearly all* the furniture was new.
i *No part of* the process is unchecked.
j *The entire* garden was redesigned.
k *A small minority of* houses had power cuts.

2 Now match the statements **1–4** below with the statements **a–f** which have the same meaning. Some will have more than one answer.

1 July was slightly hotter than August.
2 July was nowhere nearly as hot as August.
3 July was substantially hotter than August.
4 July was not quite as hot as August.

a August was much cooler than July.
b August was much hotter than July.
c August was not quite as hot as July.
d August was a lot cooler than July.
e August was slightly hotter than July.
f August was marginally cooler than July.

Now check your answers to these exercises. When you have done so, decide whether you wish to change any of your answers to Reading Passage 1. Then check your answers to Reading Passage 1 in the Key.

READING PASSAGE 2

You should spend about 20 minutes on **Questions 14–26**, *which are based on Reading Passage 2 on the following pages.*

Questions 14–20

Reading Passage 2 has seven sections, **A–G**.

Choose the correct heading for sections **A–G** *from the list of headings below.*

List of Headings
i   The main features of smart ways to provide services
ii   Possible examples of the best smart cities
iii The growth of urbanization
iv   The birth of a new global concept
v   Smart cities as attractive places to live and work
vi   Another important criterion for selecting a smart city
vii An explanation rather than a definition of the smart city concept
viii An analysis of present and future economic growth
ix   The importance of outcomes and performance
x   How the developing world copies the West

14 Section A

15 Section B

16 Section C

17 Section D

18 Section E

19 Section F

20 Section G

A The focus on making cities work efficiently for the benefit of their inhabitants, in so-called 'Smart Cities', is a concept that has come into being in recent years. Today, it has gained even greater prominence as individual cities around the world such as London, New York, Shanghai and Tokyo attract more and more attention internationally.

B The concept of a smart city goes way beyond the transactional relationships between citizen and the institutions that provide services in cities. It is essentially about enabling and encouraging citizens to become more active and participating members of the community, for example, providing feedback on the quality of services or the state of roads and the built environment, adopting a more sustainable and healthy lifestyle, volunteering for social activities or supporting minority groups. Furthermore, citizens need employment and smart cities are often attractive locations to live, work and visit.

But the concept is not static: there is no absolute definition of a smart city, no end point, but rather a process, or series of steps, by which cities become more 'liveable' and resilient and, hence, able to respond quicker to new challenges. Thus, a smart city should enable every citizen to engage with all the services on offer, public as well as private, in a way best suited to his or her needs. It brings together hard infrastructure, social capital including local skills and community institutions, and (digital) technologies to fuel sustainable economic development and provide an attractive environment for all.

C There are many global candidates for the title of the main smart city. Is Masdar City in the desert of Abu Dhabi with its emphasis on a carbon-free environment and its reliance on solar energy and wind power the top of the list? The city is free of cars, but it is experimenting with a network of driverless cars. Or is it Singapore with its use of real-time data to supply information about the environment and the weather? Cities such as London, Paris and Shanghai with their extensive public transport networks, and London especially with its congestion charge, might also see themselves as top contenders.

D There are five key aspects to smarter approaches to providing services, which are strongly information-driven. The first is having a modern digital infrastructure, which enables citizens to access the information they need, when they need it. A recognition that service delivery is improved by putting the citizen at the centre is the second key aspect. This involves placing the citizen's needs first, sharing management information to provide a coherent service, and offering internet service delivery where possible (at a fraction of the face-to-face cost).

The third aspect is an intelligent physical infrastructure such as transport, to enable service providers to use the full range of data both to manage service delivery on a daily basis. Another is a willingness to learn from others and experiment with new approaches and new business models. And lastly, there is a transparency of outcomes/performance, for example, city service dashboards to enable citizens to compare and challenge performance, establishment by establishment, and area by area.

E But some feel that the key attribute for a smart city – the sixth and critical criterion – is that the leadership has a clear vision of what the future city offers its people. It is a vision which has been developed in consultation with its citizens, creating an attractive environment for business across the city, so that the quality of life of all its citizens is enhanced by anticipating and meeting their needs, and so firms and people embrace the vision and want to locate and live there.

F Urbanization and economic development are two sides of the same coin. In 1800, just 2% of the world's population was urbanized. By 1900, this had risen to 13%; in 2000, the figure had reached 47%; and in 2008, it passed 50%. On current trends it is estimated to be 60% in 2030; 70% or even 75% in 2050; and virtually all this growth will take place in the developing world as it imitates Western Europe and North America.

G According to the McKinsey Global Institute's extensive study of global cities, 80% of global GDP is generated in cities with 50% in the 380 major cities of the developed world and 10% in the largest 220 cities of the developing world. In 2025, these top 600 cities will still be generating 60% of the growth in GDP, but their membership will have shifted East with an estimated 100 new cities entering the rankings from China alone, where the urban population is expected to rise by 200 million, to over 800 million. Some 235 million households earning more than $20,000 per annum will live in the emerging economy cities, compared to 210 million in developed region cities. Such an expanding urban middle class, with high expectations of public services and the quality of the urban infrastructure and environment, will have a profound impact on the market for smart city services.

Questions 21–25

Choose FIVE letters, A–G.

Which **FIVE** of the following features of smart cities are mentioned by the writer?

A The city has a service delivery where the citizen is at the heart of provision.
B The city allows citizens to fully engage by making all data public.
C The city possesses a smart transport system.
D The trains and buses run on time.
E There is ample opportunity for face-to-face communication.
F The public can easily access an online and up-to-date infrastructure.
G The public are open to learning from others and discovering new approaches.

Question 26

Choose the correct letter, A, B, C or D.

Which is the best title for Reading Passage 2?

A The main smart cities around the globe
B The criteria for the identification of a smart city
C The birth and growth of the smart city concept
D Smart cities of the world in the future

Before you check your answers to Reading Passage 2, go to page 116.

Questions 14–20: Matching headings

Section headings need to cover all the information in the section. You need to ask yourself if a heading relates to part of the section or the whole section. As you examine the heading itself, it is crucial that you look at the whole heading, which is normally made up of a noun phrase or a clause which is built around a central noun (growth, examples or 'how' ...). See page 112. These central nouns are crucial for understanding the text. The same applies to paragraph headings.

For Sections **A–G** on pages 113 and 114, use the statements **a–d** below to check that the headings you have chosen match the sections in the reading passage.

Section A

a   It introduces the topic of the article.
b   It contains something that relates to 'beginning'.
c   The section is about a new idea.
d   The idea is international, not local.

Section B

a   The concept is about a relationship between people and institutions.
b   The explanation begins in the second sentence.
c   A definition is not possible.
d   The concept includes various elements including attractiveness for living and working.

Section C

a   There are many examples of cities.
b   The cities are from around the world.
c   There is no clear answer about the winner.
d   The cities are all possible candidates for the top smart city.

Section D

a   There is a clear indication that a list of items is discussed.
b   Each item is marked clearly in the text.
c   It is something to do with the characteristics of a smart city.
d   These features are used as the criteria to measure a smart city.

Section E

a   An additional feature or criterion to the previous section is given.
b   It is the main global feature.
c   Smart cities being attractive places to live and work is only part of this criterion.
d   The criterion is in a separate paragraph to emphasize its importance.

Section F

a   It is about urbanization.
b   It is about the present and past.
c   It is not about economic development.
d   There is a detail about the developing world copying the West.

Section G

a   It is about economic development.
b   It is about the present and the future.
c   It is not about urbanization.
d   There is a detail about developing countries copying the West.

When you have finished the task above, decide whether you wish to change any of your answers to Questions 14–20. Then check your answers to Reading Passage 2 in the Key.

READING PASSAGE 3

*You should spend about 20 minutes on **Questions 27–40**, which are based on Reading Passage 3 below.*

Bird of Paradise:
Dancer of the jungle

THE MALE BIRD OF PARADISE with its strikingly colourful plumage is just as amazing a spectacle in the jungle of New Guinea today as it has always been. In the mating season, its bright red, yellow and blue feathers stand out against the green of the rainforest. This special bird belongs to one of the most beautiful species in the world and it has inspired many an artist. The male of the Great Bird of Paradise with its vibrant colour and fluffy, scarlet feathers, is the most spectacular-looking member of this very flamboyant species. For many Papuans the bird of paradise is a symbol of solidarity.

This bird occurs on New Guinea and its surrounding islands. Of the 43 species, 38 actually occur on the island of New Guinea itself. Six species occur on the Moluccas, a group of islands near New Guinea, and there are four species in north-east Australia. According to geologists, Australia was attached to New Guinea over 10,000 years ago, but it is now separated by the Torres Strait.

The bird of paradise is a fruit eater. Fruit is its staple diet, but seeds, insects, frogs and small reptiles are also consumed. The birds have wonderful names such as Banner Bearer, King Bird of Paradise and Lintstaartastrapia. The black crow and the jay are, in fact, related to the bird of paradise. Some species are black and resemble the black crow, but most birds of paradise are brightly coloured with long tail feathers, making them look more like a peacock than a crow. With their brightly coloured plumage, the males lure the females which are a dull brown and not at all colourful. Female birds live in small groups, but the males are usually solitary.

In the mating season, the male makes a very peculiar and very loud call, the sole purpose of which is to lure the female. To impress his mate, he shows off his lovely plumes using quite a complicated mating ritual. He repeatedly jumps from one branch to the next, and hangs upside down to make his colourful tail stand out even more. A group of females dances wildly around him. This dancing ritual always occurs on a particular spot which is known as a 'lek'. In the end, one 'lucky female' is selected for a mate.

The bird of paradise has a significant role in Papuan culture. Many tribes use the feathers for decorative headgear as well as for ceremonial dress, traditional skirts and other women's clothing. This special clothing is often passed on from one generation to the next. As birds of paradise live right at the top of trees, catching them involves a tricky procedure.

Birds of paradise have long been sought after as a status symbol. The first European to set eyes on a bird of paradise was Antonio Pigafetta from Venice, who sailed to the East Indies as an assistant of the explorer Ferdinand Magellan at the beginning of the 16th century. In 1596, the Dutch explorer, Jan Huygen van Linschoten had an enthusiastic entry in his log book about the bird of paradise. The first specimens were brought in during trade expeditions in the 16th century and it soon led to a brisk trade. During the 19th century, the first live birds were brought to Europe. Fashion designers started using the lovely feathers for ladies' hats. Between 1880 and 1890, the bird of paradise was well on its way to being decimated because of the excessive use of feathers for the hats of vain individuals. The relentless hunting continued and by the beginning of the 20th century about 50,000 birds were being traded each year.

The Dutch trade in birds of paradise began in March 1910 when Hollandia, now Jayapura, was founded. The islet Metu Debi, in the estuary at Jafeta Bay between Tobatti and Engros had been the main meeting place for bird of paradise traders around 1900. However, Hollandia only profited from the trade for a short period of time.

Initially, the trade in feathers spurred on the growth of this town, but in 1912 hunting birds of paradise became illegal and by 1922 an embargo put a stop to the trade. After this development, the numbers of birds of paradise started to rise very slowly. Local Papuans were allowed to hunt these birds to accommodate traditional customs, but these birds were no longer being exported from former Dutch New Guinea. However, after it was incorporated into Indonesia in the 1960s, the illegal trade started up again. Today, the bird of paradise is still popular across the globe because of its beauty.

Questions 27–31

Do the following statements agree with the claims of the writer in Reading Passage 3?

Write

YES	*if the statement agrees with the claims of the writer*
NO	*if the statement contradicts the claims of the writer*
NOT GIVEN	*if it is impossible to say what the writer thinks about this*

27 Male great birds of paradise have a more impressive appearance than other birds of paradise.

28 Birds of paradise are only found on the island of New Guinea.

29 Birds of paradise are close relatives of the black crow and the jay.

30 Male birds of paradise tend to live alone.

31 The purpose of the male's call during mating is to drive away other males.

Questions 32–35

Complete the sentences below.

Choose NO MORE THAN TWO WORDS AND/OR A NUMBER from the passage for each answer.

32 The part played by the bird of paradise in Papuan culture is ....

33 By the early 1900s, commercial traffic involved approximately .... birds of paradise annually.

34 .... was the location where bird traders met around the very beginning of the 20th century.

35 By 1922, the trade in birds of paradise ended as a result of an ....

Questions 36–39

Classify each event below as occurring during the

    A 16th century

    B 19th century

    C 20th century

36 the trading of the first live specimens of birds of paradise

37 the introduction of legislation to protect birds of paradise

38 the first European sighting of a bird of paradise

39 the decline in bird numbers due to fashion demands

Question 40

Choose the correct letter, A, B, C or D.

According to the writer, the bird of paradise

A does not attract as much attention as before.

B has not lost its popularity.

C has seen a decline in numbers.

D is no longer used in traditional costumes.

Now check your answers to Reading Passage 3.

Academic Writing 60 minutes

WRITING TASK 1

You should spend about 20 minutes on this task.

> *The diagrams below show the life cycle of a cotton T-shirt.*
>
> *Summarize the information by selecting and reporting the main features, and make comparisons where relevant.*

Write at least 150 words.

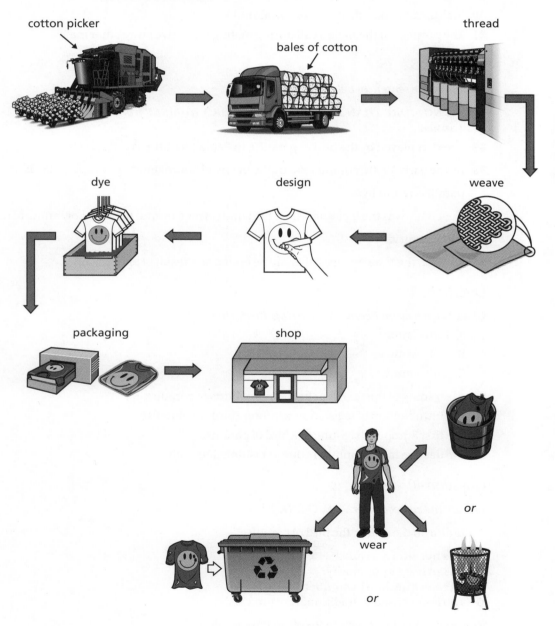

Before you write your answer to Writing Task 1, go to pages 121–122.

Tips

Writing Task 1: Describing a process

- Study the task and read the rubric carefully.
- Follow the procedure for other Writing Task 1 questions regarding the introduction, paragraphing and length, etc.
- Learn to find your way around processes, which are usually clockwise. They can sometimes contain words and phrases and symbols in the diagrams.
- Think of the tenses you will use, present simple and sometimes the present perfect.
- Make sure you use the active and passive appropriately.
- Use the agent (by ...) with passive verbs where one is indicated.

- Use appropriate linking devices and phrases (e.g. *first of all, then, next, subsequently, once, when, before*) and phrases such as *at the next stage, at the production stage*).
- Include all the steps in the processes, but learn to combine them using complex sentences.
- Be aware that the rubric says 'and make comparisons where relevant', but this is not usually possible in this type of task.
- Make sure you write an overview.
- Check your answer for mistakes.
- Keep a bank of verbs and linking devices related to processes (natural and manufacturing).

---

1 Look at the diagrams in Writing Task 1 on page 120 and answer questions **a–j** below.

   a Is the process natural, man-made or both?

   ....

   b How many stages are in the process?

   ....

   c Is it possible to write the introduction using the phrase 'The production process involved in ...'?

   ....

   d Which word can you not use in the overview: *points* or *steps* or *phases*?

   ....

   e Should the verbs in your answer be mainly in the passive or the active?

   ....

   f What kind of words is in the captions above each illustration?

   ....

   g What verbs can be used for each illustration?

   ....

   h What tense should you use in the answer/description? Why?

   ....

   i What adverbs/adverbial phrases can you use to link the stages in the description?

   ....

   j What conjunctions can you use to link the stages in the description?

   ....

2 Use the words in the noun phrases below to make sentences. You will need to change the form of some words.

1 the production of the cotton by the bushes

....

2 the harvesting of the cotton by the cotton picker

The cotton is harvested by the cotton picker.

3 the putting of the raw material into bales

....

4 the shipment of the bales to a factory

....

5 the weaving of the cotton into cloth

....

6 the design of the T-shirt

....

3 Link the sentences in Exercise 2 using the words below.

a Sentences 1 and 2:

Once ....

b Sentences 3 and 4:

Before ....

c Sentences 5 and 6:

After ....

4 Use the verbs below to make noun phrases to describe other stages in the process on page 120. Use the phrases in Exercise 2 to help you.

design: ....

manufacture: ....

produce: ....

transport: ....

sell: ....

burn: ....

recycle: ....

Now check your answers to these exercises, and then write your own answer to Writing Task 1. When you have done this, compare what you have written with the possible answers on page 152.

WRITING TASK 2

You should spend about 40 minutes on this task.

Write about the following topic:

> *More and more work is being carried out by machines in all areas of our lives.*
>
> *What are the advantages and disadvantages of this development?*

Give reasons for your answer and include any relevant examples from your own knowledge or experience.

Write at least 250 words.

Before you write your answer to Writing Task 2, go to page 124.

Writing Task 2

1 Before you write your answer to Writing Task 2 on page 123, answer the questions below.

a Does the statement describe a trend that is happening now? How do you know?

....

b What two things does the rubric ask you to focus on?

....

c Do you know any synonyms for these words or ways to paraphrase them?

....

d Is it possible to organize the essay as follows: introduction, three body paragraphs (with at least one advantage and disadvantage in each) and conclusion?

....

e Are all of the following perspectives relevant to the topic: technological, health, communication, leisure, social, employment, production, agricultural?

....

Now check your answers to this exercise, and then write your own answer to Writing Task 2.

2 When you have finished writing your answer to Writing Task 2, use the questions **a–h** below to help you check your answer.

a Does your introduction reflect the Writing Task on page 123? Or does it copy the rubric?

....

b Is your answer divided into paragraphs? Does each paragraph have a topic sentence?

....

c Does the conclusion reflect the topic sentences, the introduction and the Writing Task?

....

d Does your essay contain examples and reasons as suggested in the rubric on page 123?

....

e Does your answer contain a wide range of vocabulary and grammar structures?

....

f Does your answer contain complex sentences?

....

g Can you paraphrase any of your answer to avoid repetition?

....

h Is your answer at least 250 words and no more than about 280 words?

....

Now compare your answer with the possible answers on pages 152–153.

Speaking 11–14 minutes

PART 1 INTRODUCTION AND INTERVIEW (4–5 MINUTES)

In this part, the examiner will check your identification and you will introduce yourself.
He/She will ask you about yourself, your home, work or studies and other familiar topics.

Example

Buildings

- Which kind of buildings do you prefer – old or new? [Why?]
- In your town/city, which type of buildings are old and which type of buildings are new?
- Are buildings in the countryside the same as in the city where you live? [Why/Why not?]
- In the future, what kind of building will be most popular for living in? [Why?]

PART 2 TASK CARD (3–4 MINUTES)

Describe a rule at school that you agreed with.

You should say:
    what the rule was
    why the rule was introduced
    whether children followed the rule
and explain why you agreed with this rule.

You will have to talk about the topic for one to two minutes.
You have one minute to think about what you are going to say.
You can make some notes to help you if you wish.

Before you practise the task, go to the Further Practice and Guidance section on page 126.

PART 3 DISCUSSION (4–5 MINUTES)

Discussion topics:

Rules in everyday life

Example questions:

- What rules are most common in everyday life? Why?
- How do you think people feel about rules in everyday life?
- How would everyday life be different if there were no rules?

The impact of rules

Example questions:

- Which rules impact most on people's behaviour? Why is this?
- Would you agree that rules have a negative impact on people's creativity?
- In terms of scientific research, do you think there should be more rules and regulations about what scientists can do? Why/Why not?

Before you practise the task, go to the Further Practice and Guidance section on pages 126–127.

Part 2: Task card

Use the outline below to help you organize your answer to the task card on page 125. Complete the spaces with as much detail as you can and add examples from your own experience to make the description more interesting.

– There were many rules that I agreed with when I was at school, but the one I am going to talk about is ....

– The reason I agreed with this rule was ....

– The introduction of this rule had a number of effects on life in the school. Firstly, ... secondly, ...
and also ....

– In my opinion, this rule was a good thing, because
.... Another positive effect
was ....

Now check your answers to this exercise.

Tips

Part 3: Discussion

- Make sure you relax and concentrate on the examiner's questions.
- Be sensitive to turn-taking as this part of the Speaking component is a discussion.
- Respond to the examiner's questions appropriately. Try to paraphrase the examiner's words and try not to introduce too many unnecessary fillers.
- If you don't understand the question, tell the examiner.
- Aim to begin well.
- Develop the answer using reasons, examples and other functions such as cause and effect, purposes and your opinion.
- Avoid hesitation where possible as this will affect your score regarding fluency.
- Stick to the topic of the question and do not introduce irrelevant information and ideas.
- If you make a mistake and can correct it quickly, do so. If not, don't focus on it, just continue.
- Use a wide range of vocabulary and structures and signal your ideas by using relevant linking devices.
- Remember your ideas should be abstract rather than personal.

In Part 3, it is important to answer the questions as fully as possible, using examples from your own experience to support the points that you make.

1 Look at the items in the box below and match them with the questions in the first section of Part 3. Some items are already given.

Rules in everyday life

work regulations	pointless	disorder
lack of progress	rules of the law	inconvenient

    a *What rules are most common in everyday life? Why?*
        Example 1:   ....*school rules*............................
        Example 2:   ....
        Example 3:   ....

b *How do you think people feel about rules in everyday life?*

Example 1: ....necessary..

Example 2: ....

Example 3: ....

c *How would everyday life be different if there were no rules?*

Effect 1: ....chaos...

Effect 2: ....

Effect 3: ....

2 Now expand the notes above into full sentences to answer each question.

a ....

....

....

....

....

....

....

....

b ....

....

....

....

....

....

....

....

c ....

....

....

....

....

....

....

Now check your answers to these exercises.

Key and explanation

Test 1

PAGES 7–15
Listening Sections 1, 2 and 4

Further Practice and Guidance (pages 14–15)

Section 1: Prediction skills

Questions 1–3: Multiple-choice questions
1 T: Each of the alternatives mentions a house.
2 T: Each of the alternatives mentions jobs involved in tidying up a garden.
3 T: Each of the alternatives mentions 2 ways.
4 F: None of the alternatives mentions 3 ways.
5 T: Each of the alternatives mentions a length in metres from 15–25.
6 T: We know this from the answer in the example.

Questions 4–10: Completing a table/notes (1)
4 A number, probably relating to metres and area, i.e. square (the other entries in this column help to predict this).
   Is it a number? Is it a number and (a) word(s)? Is it a long number? How many words is it likely to be? What information is likely to be missing? What is the likely size (is it a small or large number)?
5 A noun, it could be singular, plural or uncountable.
   Is it a number or word(s)? What kind of words (see 4)? Is it likely to be singular or plural? This answer refers to the pond, can you predict what the missing detail might be?
6 A noun (it could be singular, plural or uncountable) or an adjective (as the gap is before a noun).
   Is it a number or word(s)? What kind of words (see 4)? What will the missing information tell us about the garden? Can you suggest what the missing information might be?
7 An email address, written as one word without spaces.
   What do you know about the format of email addresses? What features are likely to be included? Is some of the answer likely to be spelt out? Will it be repeated?
8 A date, including the day and month.
9 A period of time, the 'job' is the redesigning of the garden. The most likely period will be several days or weeks.
10 A mobile phone number, a sequence of approximately 11 numbers.

Section 2: Key words
11 lots of people: *crowds/crowded*
12 Argent Street/pedestrian-only: *no cars/traffic, road closed*
13 guides/city centre/help visitors: *middle of the town, dressed in, tourists*
14 profits: *proceeds/income*

Section 4: Completing a table/notes (2)
31 Key word(s): *Between 8,000 and*
   Grammar: number
32 Key word(s): *World temperature similar, weather*
   Grammar: adjective
33 Key word(s): *African, Asian, American deserts*
   Grammar: adjective, noun, noun phrase
34 Key word(s): *France, Germany, Spain*
   Grammar: noun, noun phrase
35 Key word(s): *Algeria, underground rivers, bones, animals*
   Grammar: noun, noun phrase
36 Key word(s): *flooding, storms, droughts*
   Grammar: noun, noun phrase

37 Key word(s): *wheat, barley, cultivation*
   Grammar: noun, noun phrase
38 Key word(s): *Southern European countries, production, limited*
   Grammar: noun, noun phrase
39 Key word(s): *weather changes, higher*
   Grammar: noun, noun phrase
40 Key word(s): *more, desert regions, the Sahel*
   Grammar: noun, noun phrase

The majority of the answers are nouns or noun phrases. This is because these are the parts of speech which contain the main information, and so you will often be asked to listen out for them.

PAGES 7–8
Listening Section 1

Questions 1–3
1 **A:** The designer asks *Have you just moved to the area?* and Mr Bird replies *Yes, we came here just three weeks ago.*
2 **C:** Mr Bird says *I've taken out all the rubbish and cut the grass back.*
3 **C:** Mr Bird says *It's 25 metres long.*

Questions 4–6
4 **16/sixteen square metres/meters:** The heading *Size* and the other details in the column tell you that the answer is likely to be a number and may include the word *metres*. The garden designer asks *And what size would you like to have?* before the answer is given.
5 **fish:** The word *Pond* under the heading *Garden features* gives you the key word to listen for. The designer asks *Anything else?*, i.e. *Are there any other features that you would like?* and Mr Bird says he would like a small pond, but he doesn't want any fish.
6 **vegetable:** The key word is *fence* and then *door* which goes into a *vegetable garden*. The words *herbs and potatoes, cabbage and beans, things like that* come after this, but you can't put any of them as you would need to give all the examples. The general word *vegetable* is needed here.

Questions 7–10
7 **nick@neworchard.com:** Listen for the key words for this gap: *email address*. The speaker then spells out the email address. Note that in the IELTS examination the words are not always spelt out for you.
8 **Monday (11th July):** When Mr Bird asks *can I just ask you when you can start and how long it'll take?*, you know the answers for 8 and 9 are about to be given. The garden designer says *I can start next Monday, that's the 11th* (note the link between *possible* and *can*) and Mr Bird supplies *July*.
9 **10 working days:** In answer to *how long will it take?* the designer says *it's going to take ten working days*. As the answer requires a maximum of two words and/or a number, you should write *10 working days*.
10 **07811 499466:** It's clear that this answer requires a number. The key words are: *work mobile*.

PAGES 9–10

Listening Section 2

Questions 11–14

11 **transport system:** The main presenter, Martina, says *I expect that large crowds will be using the transport system*, i.e. she predicts (expects) that there will be lots of people (*large crowds*) using the transport system. Note the word limit, and that it is important not to put *the* in the answer because it is already in the sentence.

12 **Saturday:** *Argent Street is going to be closed to all traffic including buses from 1am until 10pm on Saturday*. Note the paraphrase *closed to all traffic* for *pedestrian-only*. The key words are: *Argent Street*.

13 **yellow jackets:** The key words are: *central* (city centre) and *guides*. Following these words the speaker says (*... there'll be guides*) *who'll be in yellow jackets*.

14 **charity/(various) charities:** The speaker says: *the profits from the Food Festival* (*day's events*) *will go to* (*will be given to*) *various charities*. Note the key word *profits*.

Questions 15–18

15 **B:** The key phrase is: *in the park behind the train station*. Note that the reference to the Asian sector comes after the reference to the location: it is important to focus on chunks of information.

16 **D:** The key phrase is: *opposite the European Food Sector* and the description follows the mention of the location of the Help Point. You should make sure you listen carefully throughout, following the details that are already on the map, and be prepared to complete those that are missing.

17 **E:** The key phrase is: *The cinema is located just opposite the Latin American food display*.

18 **H:** This answer comes after the reference to the cinema further south along the street: *Cannery Hall, which is on the corner of Argent Street and Churchill Avenue*.

Questions 19 and 20

A, D in either order.
The speaker mentions the firework display last. Free food for children is mentioned, but not free food for adults. Shop discounts are mentioned, but not a film festival or music lessons.

PAGES 11–12

Listening Section 3

Questions 21–23

21 **A:** The key phrase is: *it's about 7,000 words, so that's around 2,000 words too long*.

22 **C:** Antonia says *I've been using the checklist we got in the tutorial from Dr Nakamura*. B is incorrect as she says *not the checklist you and I created ourselves*.

23 **A:** The key phrase is: *check for errors in typing and also check it from the organizational point of view*. B and C are incorrect as references are not mentioned.

Questions 24–28

For all the answers in this section, use the headings in the table (*Issue/Problem*, *Cause* and *Solution*) to help you. Also read across the table and use the headings and the key words. In each case, you need to think of synonyms and paraphrases.

24 **structure:** Cheng mentions that there is an issue with the structure.

25 **developments:** When Cheng mentions the reason (*Cause*), Antonia suggests restricting his choices to one or two perspectives like technological or cultural, or to *write about developments in the pre-Digital Age?* Note the suggestion: *why not ...?*

26 **stages:** Note Antonia says *not knowing*, which paraphrases *ignorance of* in the table.

27 **redrafting:** This is in the *Issue/Problem* column, so you know the answer is coming when Cheng says *Another problem solved!* and Antonia asks *Anything else?*

28 **summary:** Note that you hear the phrase *you could try*, which paraphrases *possibly* in the table.

Questions 29 and 30

29 **independent learning:** The key word to listen out for is *encourage*. The word *purpose* is not mentioned, but the students are discussing the aim of such essays.

30 **(the) 17th March:** The key word to listen out for is *deadline*.

PAGE 13

Listening Section 4

Questions 31–40

31 **5,500:** The answer follows the words *between 8,000 and ...*, which is the same wording as in the question.

32 **wild:** You hear *The world temperature was roughly the same as ...* (*similar to*). Then you hear *with little weather that was wild*.

33 **water:** The key phrase is: *had more water than they do now*.

34 **the UK:** You hear the list of countries in the question, so you should be prepared for the answer, which is the last in the list.

35 **earliest fields:** Algeria is introduced, and from the notes you know you will hear about rivers, bones and then the answer.

36 **livelihoods:** As in 35, the answer comes at the end of a section, so you should follow the words *flooding, storms*, etc and then be prepared for the answer. Note *our* is paraphrased by *people's*.

37 **fruit crops:** You know the answer is coming when you hear *Europe continues to warm up*. The answer *fruit crops* then follows the key words *wheat* and *barley*.

38 **agricultural goods:** The key phrase to listen out for is the mention of *countries in Southern Europe*, as the answer follows this. Note that *severely limited* has been paraphrased as *severely curtailed* in the recording.

39 **food prices:** This answer comes soon after 38, so you should be looking ahead to be aware of what the next question requires you to listen for.

40 **vegetation (cover):** The word *vegetation* is mentioned twice: *vegetation is increasing* and *increased vegetation cover*.

PAGES 16–20

Academic Reading Passage 1

Further Practice and Guidance (pages 19–20)

Questions 1–7: True/False/Not Given

Question 1

1 yes, yes
2 yes
3 yes, gold
4 no
5 no

Question 2

1 Yes: about three billion years ago.
2 yes
3 It means that the meteorite is the earliest according to records only. Yes

Question 3

1 yes
2 yes
3 yes

Question 4
1 Yes: *It was not until the time of the Spanish Conquistadors' arrival in South America in the 15th and 16th centuries that ...*
2 b
3 Yes: *... before the 15th century.*
4 Yes: b
5 prior to, previous to, previously, earlier than

Question 5
1 *little*
2 It could be both.
3 Negative: not much
4 *... to attract the interest of ...*

Questions 6 and 7
6 What was the <u>main reason</u> platinum was employed in making jewellery?
7 Is platinum <u>no longer</u> employed in the manufacture of glass?

Questions 1–7
It is worth noting that, as this is an historical text, time references and names help readers find their way around.

Note also that the questions in the three sections overlap.

1 **NOT GIVEN:** The text says that platinum is r*arer than gold, in fact some 30 times rarer,* but there is no information about it being the *least common* metal in the world.

2 **TRUE:** The answer lies in the third sentence of the first paragraph. The statement in the exercise is about the *first known meteorite*, while the text talks about *the earliest recorded* meteorite. In other words, there may have been meteorites before this, but we do not know about them.

3 **TRUE:** The answer is in the third sentence of the second paragraph. The words *Incas, civilizations* and *South America* help to locate the information. The text says *the most famous*, which is paraphrased by *more well known* (than other) in the statement.

4 **FALSE:** The answer is in the fourth sentence of the second paragraph. Note the time phrase in the text *It was not until the time of the Spanish Conquistadors' arrival in South America in the 15th and 16th centuries that* and the corresponding phrase in the statement *before the 15th century.*

5 **FALSE:** The answer lies in the first sentence of the third paragraph. The text emphasizes the fact that *it began to attract the interest of scientists in Europe.* The statement says *took little notice,* which contradicts the information in the text.

6 **NOT GIVEN:** The answer is in the last two sentences of the fourth paragraph. The text mentions that *platinum is desirable in jewellery for various reasons,* but there is no information as to whether the fact that it was hard-wearing was the main reason platinum was used in jewellery.

7 **FALSE:** The answer is in the third sentence of the fifth paragraph. The phrases *The current manufacture of glass, as in the past,* and *are all reliant on platinum* contradict the information in the statement *is no longer employed in the manufacture of glass.*

Questions 8–10
8 **cumbersome:** The answer is in the third sentence of the third paragraph. Note it is the last adjective in the sentence.
9 **torch:** The answer is in the fifth sentence of the third paragraph. The word *high-temperature* helps to locate the information.
10 **store of value:** The answer is in the first sentence of the fourth paragraph.

Questions 11–13
A, C, F in any order.

The answers are in the last three paragraphs. The answer A is in the whole of the sixth paragraph; C is in the second sentence of the sixth paragraph; and F is in the first sentence of the fifth paragraph.

B is incorrect, because the text mentions in the last sentence of the sixth paragraph that platinum was discovered in South Africa in the 20th century (mid-1920s). As for D, there is no mention of current production of platinum increasing in Russia in paragraphs six and seven. E contradicts the information in the last sentence of the text.

PAGES 21–25
Academic Reading Passage 2

Further Practice and Guidance (pages 24–25)

Questions 14–20: Matching information
Question 14
1 yes
2 it is likely that
3 *making things out of dough, putting on dressing-up clothes, playing around with sand*

Question 15
1 purpose: to explain/define the words *creative learning.* This is likely to be in a sentence towards the beginning of the paragraph.
2 The rest of the paragraph: one sentence defines *creative learning*, and this is followed by how it needs to be promoted.
3 definition/elaboration

Question 16
1 *every six weeks*
2 *assessed*

Question 17
1 describe a process
2 Yes: engineers/engineering
3 *they investigate a problem, They start with, then think, and then apply.* Four steps are described.
4 yes

Question 18
1 *kids*
2 negative
3 yes

Question 19
1 To describe/question a suggestion about measurement (of creativity).
2 *suggestion/could*
3 *be included*
4 *evaluating*
5 no

Question 20
1 Yes: teachers' view(s)
2 Yes: creative approaches, in the classroom
3 need, needs, needy, necessary, necessity; essential, required, crucial

Questions 14–20
14 **A:** The answer is in the first sentence of paragraph A: *the chances are that you'll see children at play: making things out of dough ..., putting on dressing-up clothes or playing around with sand.*

15 **D:** The answer is in the whole paragraph, but specifically the first and second sentences.

16 **G:** The answer is in the second sentence of the paragraph (*every six weeks*). To locate the information, a paraphrase of *frequency* and words related to *assessment* need to be looked for.

17 **E:** The answer is in the whole paragraph, but begins with the word *engineers*. In matching information to paragraphs, the information may relate to part of a paragraph, a chunk of the paragraph or the whole paragraph.

18 **G:** The answer is in the third sentence: *terrified of taking risks, of getting something wrong*. This is paraphrased by *reluctant to make mistakes* in the statement. Note the instructions in the rubric, so you can use any letter more than once.

19 **H:** The answer is in the first sentence (*evaluating*).

20 **B:** The answer is in the second sentence and is a view put forward by teachers.

Questions 21–24

21 **imaginations run free:** The answer is in the last sentence of paragraph A. The answer comes after the text mentions that children *learn social skills and teamwork*. Note the paraphrase *allows children to see what happens once their* compared to *discover what can occur when they let their* in the text.

22 **to the test:** The answer is in the second sentence of paragraph B. Note the paraphrase: *its emphasis on* and *is stressed*.

23 **broadcast model:** The answer is in the last sentence of paragraph D. Note the paraphrases *argued* and *advocated*, *shift* and *moving away from*.

24 **desperate:** The answer is in the last sentence of paragraph F.

Questions 25–27

Note that the multiple-choice stems in this section identify the paragraph where the answer is found.

25 **A:** The answer is in the last sentence of paragraph G. No mention is made of alternative B and C. As regards D, paragraph G mentions facts, but the point is made that it's not about *learning essential facts*, but about *reciting* them.

26 **C:** The answer is in the last sentence of paragraph I. The third sentence says: *'The very first thing that needs to change is that pupils need to be encouraged to question the teacher,' said one participant*. This does not mean that pupils give teachers 'orders', so A is not possible. As regards B, there is no mention of pupils being given more control, and D is not mentioned.

27 **B:** The answer is in the third sentence of paragraph J. A is not about 'autonomy' as it involves dealing with problems with the help of other children. C is related to 'ambiguity' in the fourth sentence. D is not mentioned.

PAGES 26–28
Academic Reading Passage 3

Questions 28–32

28 **NO:** The answer is in the last sentence of the first paragraph: *why some dunes …*, which contradicts *All* in the statement. Note that the rubric is testing claims, i.e. something that the writer says is true. It is a good strategy to collect examples of the types of sentences that are used in claims. The same can be done for True/False/Not Given statements. This way the patterns of the sentences can be seen.

29 **YES:** The answer is in the first sentence of the second paragraph. The word *world* helps to locate the relevant part of the text. Note that the phrase *are not common* in the statement paraphrases *(only sing) in a few areas (across the globe)* in the text.

30 **NO:** The answer is in the last sentence of the second paragraph. The text gives an explanation with two examples of mechanisms that make the sand sing: *People can set the sand in motion themselves* and then another way, *or, more creepily, the wind can create avalanches or landslides, producing a sudden, loud*

chorus. It is important to read before and after the details in the text that seem to give the answer.

31 **YES:** The answer is in the first sentence of the third paragraph: *in the more stable layers of sand inside the dunes*. Note the phrase *Scientists previously thought* which is paraphrased by *In the past, it was believed that*.

32 **NOT GIVEN:** The crucial word in the statement is <u>unique</u>. The writer does not mention anywhere whether the sound produced by the sand grains in the Omani dunes is unique compared to the sound produced by sand in other areas.

Questions 33–37

33 **F:** The answer is in the first sentence of the sixth paragraph (*lab*). The answers for this and the next four questions are found in the sixth and seventh paragraphs. The heading *Lab experiments on the Omani sand* helps to locate the relevant part of the text where the answers are found. Sometimes, there is no heading above the summary in the exam. Sometimes, the information in the summary is not in order, but in this summary, it is.

34 **H:** The answer is in the second sentence of the sixth paragraph: *… and calculating the sand's vibrations with sensors*. Note that in summaries, the same words and phrases may be used in the summary itself and the list of words and phrases may be the same as in the reading passage.

35 **D:** The answer is in the last sentence of the sixth paragraph. The clue is in the word *size* (numbers or adjectives) and *separated out* (*isolated*).

36 **I:** The answer is in the first sentence of the seventh paragraph: *The researchers then compared the sound*. Note the use of another word in the word family of *compare* (*compared/comparison*) to create the paraphrase.

37 **A:** The answer is in the last sentence of the seventh paragraph: *of some significance (in the tone the dunes sing in)*.

Questions 38–40

38 **more explanation:** The answer is in the second sentence of the last paragraph. The name *Patitsas* helps to locate the answer as does the word *theory*.

39 **stationary sand:** The answer is in the second and third sentences of the last paragraph. The text says that *flowing sand* (sliding sand) *needs a thin layer of stationary sand underneath it to make a sound*, and that these flowing sands vibrate when moving across them.

40 **sound volume:** The answer is in the last sentence of the reading passage: *Once you have this* (intensified vibration) *the sound volume of the vibration will be large*.

PAGES 29–32
Academic Writing Task 1

Further Practice and Guidance (pages 30–32)

1
a viii b v c vii d iii e ii f viii g vi h vi i iv
j iv k vii l i

2 yes

3
f There was a dramatic rise in fruit sales.
g There was a plunge/dramatic drop in the number of people attending the lectures.
h The share price fell dramatically.
i There was a substantial drop in share prices, followed by a flat trend in prices.
j After the number of people settling in the city declined significantly, it remained stable.
k There was a dip in the number of houses sold.
l The number of children visiting the zoo declined gradually.

Plummet (sentence **i**) cannot be changed into a noun.

4
1 d/e   2 a/c   3 b/f   4 f   5 d/e   6 c   7 a   8 a   9 f
10 d

6
Checklist

1 Yes: it is 176 words. It is appropriate for the task. It is important to aim for more than 150, e.g. between 160–185 words. If the answer is too long, it may be penalized for not summarizing.
2 Yes: there are four paragraphs: an introduction, two paragraphs describing the data and an overview.
3 It summarizes and compares it with an overview at the end.
4 It paraphrases the rubric with only a few essential words mentioned again such as *access, internet, households, frequency* and the dates being used again.
5 Yes: in the last paragraph. Note it is possible to include the overview in the first paragraph or as the first sentence of the second paragraph.
6 Yes: the data is summarized by, for example, giving the values at the beginning and the end of periods. It is not necessary to add information about every year.
7 Yes: in the first line of the third paragraph: *There seems to be a correlation between the increase in access and the frequency of internet access.*
8 Yes: for example, *proportion, along with, as regards, grew gradually, approximately/about/around, climbed, at a faster pace, rise, the latter, mirrored, increase, correlation, daily, steady decline.*
9 Yes: *By comparison, broadband access climbed at a faster pace up to 2010–11, going up from about 40% to 68% respectively, while the rise in the latter period mirrored the overall access with an increase to about 74%.*
10 no

Possible answers

Version 1

> *The charts provide information about the proportion of Australian households that have access to the internet along with the frequency of access between 2006–07 and 2012–13.*
>
> *As regards general internet access, broadband and non-broadband, the proportion of households grew gradually from approximately 70% to around 77% in 2006–07 and 2012–13 respectively. By comparison, broadband access climbed at a faster pace up to 2010–11, going up from about 40% to 68% respectively, while the rise in the latter period mirrored the overall access with an increase to about 74%.*
>
> *There seems to be a correlation between the increase in access and the frequency of internet access. The proportion of those accessing the internet daily rose from about 63% to 83%. By contrast, although there was a steady decline in access at least once per week from around 30% to 20%, the trend in access at least once a month remained flat (approximately 1%).*
>
> *Overall, there is a clear upward trend in internet access and internet use with the proportion of those with broadband access on the rise.*

Word count: 176 words

Comments

This is a good possible answer. The introduction paraphrases the rubric in the Writing Task. The main data are covered and there is an attempt to summarize (*the rise in the latter period mirrored the overall access with an increase to about 74%; There seems to be a correlation between the increase in access and the frequency of*

internet access and then explains using specific data), and a clear overview (*Overall, there is a clear upward trend in internet access and internet use with the proportion of those with broadband access on the rise.*).

There is a wide range of structures (*access climbed at a faster pace, going up from about, the rise in the latter period mirrored*) and vocabulary (*pace, mirrored, correlation*), and the answer contains complex sentences to combine information (*By comparison, broadband access climbed at a faster pace up to 2010–11, going up from about 40% to 68% respectively, while the rise in the latter period mirrored the overall access with an increase to about 74%.*).

Version 2

> *The graphs show the percentage of households with internet and broadband access in Australia, together with frequency of internet access, between 2006–07 and 2012–13.*
>
> *As regards general internet access, broadband and non-broadband, the proportion of households grew gradually from approximately 70% to around 77% in 2006–07 and 2012–13 respectively. Broadband access climbed faster to 2010–11, going up from about 40% to 68% respectively and the rise in the latter period was similar to the overall access. It also increased to about 74%.*
>
> *As regards the frequency of internet access, the proportion of those accessing the internet daily rose from about 63% to 83%. In addition, access at least once per week steadily fell from around 30% to 20% and the trend in access at least once a month was flat (approximately 1%).*
>
> *Overall, there is a clear upward trend in internet access and internet use, and the proportion of those with broadband access rose.*

Word count: 154 words

Comments

This is not as good an answer as Version 1. The introduction copies the rubric in the Writing Task, which may affect the final score. The main data are covered, but they are listed and there is no attempt to summarize except for the overview (*Overall, there is a clear upward trend in internet access and internet use, and the proportion of those with broadband access rose.*). The sentences largely follow the same (Subject, Verb, Object) pattern.

There is not a wide range of structures or vocabulary, and the answer does not attempt to combine information by using complex sentences.

PAGE 33
Academic Writing Task 2

Possible answers

Version 1

> *In the modern world, children have a less active lifestyle than in the past. While some people feel that parents should take the lead in tackling this problem through the encouragement of regular exercise, others argue that schools should do so. Personally, I think that both should share the burden.*
>
> *Some people think that parents have a duty to ensure their children have regular exercise, because they are the children's main role models. What they say and do has a major impact on children's actions. If, for example, children see their parents going to the park doing exercise, they are more likely to do the same.*

Other people, however, argue that schools should bear the main responsibility, as children spend most of their early life at school. For example, schools can train children in different sports such as swimming. They add that parents cannot do this, because they are at work or do not have the facilities to organize these activities. Another argument is that physical education classes can help children concentrate more in other lessons.

I personally feel that it is a matter of shared responsibility. Take exercise at school, for example. If children are taught to do sport such as tennis, and then they do not do anything similar at home, they are not likely to adopt a keen interest in exercise. What is more, it is important for parents to take an interest in their children's sporting activities as this will encourage children to want to do more.

As we have seen, both groups have an important role to play in encouraging children to exercise regularly, and so it should be a matter of shared responsibility.

Word count: 279 words

Comments

This is an example of a good answer. The introduction paraphrases the rubric and indicates what the answer will discuss. The answer covers the three parts of the rubric (view 1 in paragraph 2, view 2 in paragraph 3, and the writer's opinion in paragraph 4). The answer is well organized and there is a clear connection between each body paragraph, and the introduction and the conclusion, and between the whole question and the Writing Task. For example, each body paragraph has a clear topic sentence in the first sentence. There are reasons (e.g. *because they are the children's main role models*) and examples (*If, for example, children see their parents going to the park doing exercise*), with complex sentences (*While some people feel that parents should take the lead in tackling this problem through the encouragement of regular exercise, others …/They add that parents cannot do this, because they are at work or do not have the facilities to organize these activities*) and a range of vocabulary (*ensure, a major impact on, facilities, keen*) and structures (*both should share, they are more likely to do the same*).

Version 2

Some people think that parents should be responsible for encouraging their children to take regular exercise. Others argue that the main responsibility for encouraging children to do so should lie with schools. Personally, I think that both should take responsibility for encouraging children to take exercise.

Parents should make sure that children have regular exercise. They are the children's main role models and have an effect on their children. If children see their parents going to the park doing exercise, they will do the same. If parents sit at home, children will copy them. This is not good for the children.

Other people, however, argue that schools should be mainly responsible. This is because children spend most of their early life at school. Schools train children in different sports. And parents cannot do this, because they are at work and they do not have the facilities to organize activities. And physical education classes can help children concentrate more in other lessons.

I personally feel that it is a matter of shared responsibility. In school, if children are taught to do sport, and then do not do anything similar at home, they will not adopt an interest in exercise. What is more, it is important for parents to take an interest in their children's sporting activities as this will encourage children to want to do more.

As we have seen, both groups have an important role to play in encouraging children to exercise regularly, and so it should be a matter of shared responsibility.

Word count: 253 words

Comments

This answer is clearly not as good as Version 1. The introduction copies the rubric, which may affect the final score, and while it indicates what the answer will discuss, it is very repetitive (e.g. *encouraging*). The answer, however, does address the three parts of the rubric (view 1 in paragraph 2, view 2 in paragraph 3 and the writer's opinion in paragraph 4). The answer is well organized and there is a clear connection between each body paragraph and the introduction and the conclusion, and between the whole question and the Writing Task. For example, each body paragraph has a clear topic sentence in the first sentence.

The answer is very general, however. There are few clear reasons and examples with some complex sentences (*If children see their parents going to the park doing exercise, they will do the same*; *If parents sit at home, children will copy them*), but these are repetitive and overall there is a narrow range of vocabulary and structures.

PAGES 34–35
Speaking Part 1

Further Practice and Guidance (page 35)

1
Hobbies
Examples: *cycling, computer games, reading, photography, travelling, video games*
Reasons: *fitness, enjoyment, relaxation, personal advancement*
Frequency: *daily/weekly/monthly, often/occasionally/seldom/once a …/every …/rarely*
Vocabulary: *pastime/recreation, enjoyable/interesting/stimulating/rewarding/satisfying, spare/free time*

Family
Examples: *parents, children, siblings, in-laws, extended family*
Reasons: [*I like them because …*] *helpful, supportive, funny*
Frequency: [*I see/contact them …*] *frequently, in person, by Skype™, by text*
Vocabulary: *relatives, generations, relationship*

Studying
Examples: *past achievements, current study, future plans*
Reasons: *career path, further study plans, personal advancement*
Frequency: *see* Hobbies *above*
Vocabulary: *course, qualification, requirement, college/university, cost/fee/grant*

Ambition
Examples: *short-term, long-term, career dreams, personal dreams*
Reasons: *successful at university, exciting career, happy life*
Vocabulary: *aspiration, desire, hope/wish/dream*

Buildings
Examples: *old, new, type of architecture*
Reasons: *purpose, attractive, modern, old-fashioned*
Vocabulary: *ancient, modern/contemporary, purpose-built, architect, tourist attraction*

2
Hobbies:
What do you enjoy doing when you have free time? Why?
Family:
How often do you speak to/see other members of your family? How? Why?
Studying:
What is the most important qualification you have gained so far?

Ambition:
What is the most important goal in your life at the moment?
Buildings:
Tell me about one of the most important buildings in
your country.

PAGES 34–35
Speaking Part 2

Further Practice and Guidance (page 35)

Possible answers:
Time: teenager
Person: history teacher
Place: secondary school
Help: understand history-related events
How I felt: grateful, more confident

Note you will not have time to write more notes than this. If you
do write more, it is possible you will read them rather than
glancing at them. This will affect your fluency.

Test 2

PAGE 36
Listening Section 1

Questions 1–10

1 **whole family:** Ricky asks what Daniella would like to know, and she asks *could you tell me how much it costs to cover the whole family for a year?*

2 **9:** The heading *Ages* and the information for the boy and the ages of the parents indicate the number is not very big.

3 **primary (school):** The word *teacher* helps to predict the answer. The heading *Occupations* is the key word to listen for.

4 **(major) illnesses:** The word *past* is the key word and so is the word *previous: And in the past, have any of you had any major illnesses, like …?*

5 **hospital stays:** The key words to listen for are *plan* and *cover*. Daniella tells Ricky she would like *cover for the dentist, the optician, and the doctor and hospital stays.*

6 **alternative:** Ricky asks *What about alternative therapies?* and then Daniella asks if they're covered in the comprehensive plan. Ricky also gives *acupuncture* and *physiotherapy* as examples of alternative therapies.

7 **73.59:** At the beginning of this part of the test, Daniella asks about *the cost* and Ricky gives the amount.

8 **PB663885FJ:** It's important not to confuse the letters *PB* (for *BP*) and *FJ* (for *SG*), and to listen carefully for the numbers. The key word is *reference.*

9 **2/two months:** Ricky points out that there is a discount *Oh, and I should mention the discount.*

10 **in advance:** The word *Payment* in the test and the words *one year* and *monthly* tell you to listen for information about frequency of payment. Ricky says *You can pay… for the year in advance or … each month.*

PAGE 37
Listening Section 2

Questions 11–13
D, E, G in any order.

The speaker mentions the *internationally famous golf course* at the beginning. There is then a gap before the *coffee shops* and then the *bookshops* are mentioned. Note the speaker says *nor will you find any fast-food restaurants.* A *literary festival* is mentioned but not a *film festival.* Note the items in the list are not in the order they are mentioned in the test.

Questions 14–17
Questions 14–17 are in the order they occur in the test, but A–G are jumbled. In this section, you might want to put a dot next to the items A–G as you select them.

14 **E:** You need to listen for the key names of the beaches as they are mentioned. The speaker says *and parking is not easy. There's no car park, so visitors have to leave their vehicles along the roads approaching the beach.*

15 **A:** The speaker says *This is one of the reasons why Sandy Beach is very suitable for families.* Parking is not difficult at this beach as there's *a huge car park.*

16 **D:** The speaker says *It's very popular with surfers.* It is also mentioned that *This beach is not really for families with children or older people.* So A is not suitable.

17 **C:** The speaker says *The fourth beach is Little Cove, an area of outstanding natural beauty.*

Questions 18–20

18 **old houses:** The key words are: *tourists* and *countryside.* The speaker says *There are villages with old houses to visit.*

19 **(the) woodland(s):** You know the answer is coming when you hear *cliff top walks along the coast,* which is in the previous bullet point. The speaker goes on to say *walks in the woodlands* as the next feature. The singular or plural form is possible, though *woodlands* is mentioned.

20 **canoeing, swimming** in either order: The key words are: *water sports* (*river activities*). Both words are necessary for a correct answer.

PAGES 38–40
Listening Section 3

Further Practice and Guidance (pages 39–40)

Questions 21–23: Answering questions

21 one, noun, less, likely
Many commodities are one word, but some are two words like *iron ore.*

22 nouns, and, helps

23 noun phrase or noun, an adjective + a noun, helps

Questions 24–27: Following a table

1 yes   2 horizontally   3 yes   4 yes
5 a number   6 percentages   7 smaller
8 yes   9 a noun   10 a number

Questions 28–30: Completing sentences

28 Yes: she wants to hold something such as notes, cards, paper or a script.

29 yes

30 Yes: this answer is difficult to predict.

Questions 21–23

21 **sugar:** Tanya says *At first, I was going to do it on sugar in the future.* The key word in the question is *first.* The question word *Which* indicates that the answer is a noun/noun phrase. It's clear it's not *corn* from Question 23 and the heading for Questions 24–27.

22 **metal(s) (and) oil:** The answer to this follows on closely from Question 21. Note that in the question there is an indication that a different person (*Carlo*) gives the answer. Both words are necessary for the answer to be correct, but the word *and* could be left out. Note that *metal* is also correct.

23 **population growth:** The answer to this is again a noun/noun phrase, and comes after the words the speaker talks about *price increases* (*rise in prices*) and a *cause* (*because of*).

Questions 24–27

24 **50/fifty:** Logically, all the information about the United States is given first. The % symbol shows that the answer is a number. Care needs to be taken to concentrate between the answer to Question 23 and this question. The heading *Corn exporters* helps to alert the listener that the information for the table is about to be given.

25 **114:** The patterns of the answers in the columns give a clue to the nature of the answer: a number. It is likely that the answer is not large given the relative sizes of the United States and the UK. The information *EU – 3%* is also an indication of the size of the number. Care needs to be taken not to confuse 114 with 140 or 104.

26 **potential:** The adjective before 26 *huge* shows the answer is a noun not a number.

27 **40/forty:** The % symbol shows that the answer you need is a number: *… it has about 40% of the world's uncultivated cropland.*

Questions 28–30

28 **script:** Tanya says *But how can I stop myself reading from a script?* and then *I'll be so nervous if I don't have one to read from.*

29 **2/two minutes:** the word *time* helps to indicate the nature of the answer. Note the change of speaker also helps. Carlo says *To help make myself focus, I've put the slides on a timer, so I have only two minutes per slide.* Notice how Question 29 paraphrases this information.

30 **animation/special features:** It is not easy to predict the answer here. Carlo asks *what about animation? Is it OK to use special features like that?* And then the tutor agrees *By all means, yes.*

PAGES 41–44
Listening Section 4

Further Practice and Guidance (pages 43–44)

Questions 31–34: Multiple-choice questions

1

Question 31
1 No: *The government gave money to*
2 Yes: *(to) expand/(to) help/(to) promote*
3 Yes: *expand, help* and *promote* are positive verbs.
4 Yes: it could be rephrased as *The Fashion Design Project was given money by the government to*

Question 32
5 Yes: *(cause) has increased* (effect)
6 Yes: *collaboration* – cooperation; *other departments and outside companies* – other agencies; *has increased* – has made something bigger

Question 33
7 No
8 No
9 No: *result in* follows the pattern: cause → effect; *result from* follows the pattern: effect → cause

Question 34
10 Yes: *didn't function properly*
11 No
12 Yes: *the fabrics ... tore easily/felt ... too simple in design/did not work well*
13 No

2

Are there other ways of expressing the words in the stem?
Are there other words that come from words in the stem or options?
Is there a relationship between the stem and the options?
Does the stem contain a problem?
Does the stem contain a solution?
Does the stem or the options contain examples?

3

Note that paraphrasing may include synonyms, changes in grammar and the use of different words in a word family.
31 c: *gave money to*
32 a: *Collaboration*
33 b: *Raising the profile*
      d: *has resulted in*
34 e: *prototypes*
      f: *didn't function properly*

Questions 35–40: Completing notes
36 *It's about design not just about something else like [the way it works].*
37 *There are several main challenges like the fact that the public may not want technology in their clothes, and the extra cost*

may put people off. So it is necessary to create clothes that work, get the attention of the public and are [something positive].

38 *People may be weary of new technology. So the introduction of any new product into the market needs to be done at the appropriate [something to do with moment].*

39 *This means that we need to use [something in the media] that is appealing.*

40 *There are drawbacks like possible obsession with data, not leaving home without tech-wearables, and we also have to be careful about the clothes and technology being destroyed after people dirty them and they need [something].*

Questions 31–34

31 **B:** The speaker says *Design Project, which is partly funded by a government grant,* which paraphrases the stem. The speaker then introduces the purpose with the words *in order to* (*help establish links between ...*). A and C are not correct as there is nothing about expansion or promotion here. Also notice the word *specifically* in the Listening test.

32 **A:** The speaker describes the different teams he and his colleagues are working with (*inside the university, not just those in the Technology Institute, but also Sports, Science and Health* and *the two local tech companies we're involved with*). And then describes the main *benefit* (*effect*) of this *cooperation* (*collaboration*): *has led to the products that we're working on appealing much more to the commercial world.*

33 **C:** The stem contains the cause of *raising the profile* (*enhanced reputation*) and the options contain possible results (*consequence*). Of the result, the speaker says *we've received increased research funding.* So the effect is not about *cuts* (A), nor is it about *alarm* (B).

34 **C:** The speaker says *Early examples of products* (*prototypes*) *we made were clumsy and not very attractive and awkward to wear.* A reason: *as it was difficult to put the technology and garments such as shirts or vests together,* i.e. *the technology did not work well with the clothes.* There is nothing about tearing (A) or the clothes being too simple in design (B).

Questions 35–40

35 **accessories:** The key words are in the heading *Fashion items* and the words *Focus on* (*concentrating on*). Note the general noun *items* in the heading.

36 **function:** This answer comes shortly after the answer for Question 35. The speaker says: *that will appeal to the general public because of their design, not just their function.* The key words here are *attraction* (*appeal*), *general public* and *design*.

37 **inexpensive/cheap:** Note the general noun *Challenges* in the heading, which is the first key word (*there's no doubt that there are challenges*). The speaker introduces the *Need* (*what we need to do ... is*), and the answer comes after the word *public*.

38 **time:** The key words are: *technology-weary, introduction* (*introducing*) and *appropriate* (*right*). As the word *appropriate* is a synonym of *right*, care needs to be taken not to add the word *right* to the answer as this would be marked wrong. Also note the rubric (*one word*).

39 **advertising:** The key word is *appealing* (*catching the eye,* i.e. attracting people's attention).

40 **cleaning:** The answer comes towards the end: *nor the technology are destroyed through cleaning.* So it is important to concentrate and follow the succession of key words: *obsession with data, tech-wearable* and *destruction of* (*destroyed*).

Note that it is necessary to be able to expand the notes quickly and automatically *in your head* in the Listening test.

PAGES 45–49
Academic Reading Passage 1

Further Practice and Guidance (pages 48–49)

Questions 1–5: Matching headings to paragraphs
relationship: link, connection, correlation, association
need: necessity, requirement
strategies: techniques, methods, ways, approaches, measure, 'how'
ability: aptitude, skill, capacity, capability

Paragraph B
a Yes: *a good education* and *creativity/being creative*
b Yes: *But success for young people today requires a range of attributes, some of which may be possible to teach and develop. Yet many, if not most, are innate.*
c Yes: writers usually do this. The principle is the same in academic writing, speaking and listening. Think about introductions and topic sentences in essays.
d Yes: *Just like having a good education, it seems that this noticing or seeing in creativity can be taught.*

Paragraph C
a The second sentence
b *but these, like being well-educated or creative, are not enough to guarantee success. What is probably more necessary than these qualities … .* Often, the first sentence of a paragraph links back to the previous paragraph, and then the new idea is introduced.
c It explains the word *vision* in the second sentence.
d Yes: it gives extra information about *vision*. The words which show this are *It also includes.*

Paragraph D
a Yes: the words are *further strengths … necessary to 'develop a vision' … .*
b *self-motivation* and *perseverance*: they are mentioned at the beginning of the first sentence.
c Yes: they are *inextricably linked*
d Yes: *These are essential forces that propel successful people, …*
e It is just additional information.

Paragraph E
a yes
b Yes: *Self-motivation can also be initiated by … .* Notice the word *also.*
c Yes: iii (*Strategies*)

Paragraph F
a yes
b *being proactive*
c Yes: *There is a tendency generally for …, whereas …*

Questions 1–5
One important piece of information about the organization of paragraphs is that the topic sentence, i.e. the sentence which summarizes what is in the paragraph, does not always come in the first sentence. Moreover, reading the first and last sentences in paragraphs to work out the overall meaning of a paragraph does not always work.

1 **iv:** The last two sentences of paragraph A help you to understand what is coming next in the reading passage: *But success for young people today requires a range of attributes, some of which may be possible to teach and develop. Yet many, if not most, are innate.* The writer will look at 'teachable' and then 'innate' attributes (i.e. those we are born with). Education is the first teachable attribute in the first sentence and being creative is

introduced in the second sentence. Note the word *two* is mentioned in heading **i**, but there is nothing in paragraph B about driving success.

2 **ii:** The writer introduces the idea that some attributes (e.g. *being ambitious* and *having talent*) cannot be taught and then mentions another attribute *having a vision* in the second sentence, which is the focus of the paragraph. It is important to ask yourself what the purpose of the paragraph is: to talk about having a vision. So the answer cannot be **vii**, because the paragraph is not about a comparison of talent and ambition.

3 **i:** The first and second sentences give the answer. We have the word *Two* and then we have *Two qualities*: *self-motivation* and *perseverance* in the first sentence. In the second sentence, we have: *These are essential forces that propel successful people.* Learn to concentrate on much wider information than just one or two words. You can check the answer further down the paragraph: *It is difficult to separate the two qualities.* Reading the beginning of sentences as you glance through a paragraph will give a clue about the organization; especially if the subject or focus changes. The answer cannot be **vi** as the heading is too general and the focus is on two specific qualities that drive success.

4 **iii:** The paragraph talks about different ways to increase self-motivation, i.e. bribing oneself and limiting time spent working on something. These match with heading **iii** as they are strategies to develop self-motivation.

5 **v:** The answer is again at the beginning of the paragraph in the first sentence: *Part of self-motivation is being proactive rather than reactive, that is doing things first rather than responding to other people's actions.* The writer explains what being *proactive* means, and the rest of the paragraph discusses this.

Questions 6–10
It is important to be clear about the rubric or instructions: the questions here are about the views of the writer. So something may be mentioned in the reading passage, but the writer does not comment on it, or contradicts or agrees with it. The statements 6–10 are in the order the information occurs in the text. It is also useful to collect categories of words such as words related to quantity as they occur in statements like these and True/False/Not Given statements.

6 **YES:** Question 6 feels very general as the others are all related to specific attributes or qualities. It is therefore logical to look in paragraph A for something about *youth, today, unfairly judged* and *outdated standards*: *The young are often unjustly measured by the media and parents against knowledge-focused criteria that are more relevant to previous generations than to the modern digital age.* Note the opinion in the words *unfairly judged.*

7 **NO:** Note that the statement *The necessary attributes for success can be learnt* implies that *all* attributes needed for success can be learnt. Contrast this with *some, many* and *not most* in: *But success for young people today requires a range of attributes, some of which may be possible to teach and develop. Yet many, if not most, are innate.*

8 **NOT GIVEN:** Both qualities are mentioned in paragraph B, but the writer does not say what he thinks. He does quote what some people think, however: … *attribute that to some people is much more important than education, and it is often cited as the single most important quality in success.* It is important not to confuse what the writer thinks and what some people think.

9 **NOT GIVEN:** The answer is in paragraph C: *Other attributes such as being ambitious and having talent cannot be taught.* The writer does not, however, claim that these attributes cannot be nourished [note the difference in meaning between *taught* and *nourished*].

10 **YES:** The answer is in paragraph D: *In fact, failure is useful because it can help sharpen people's talents, especially once they have learnt how it can be dealt with.*

Questions 11–13

Note the rubric: not *one* word but *two*, and not more than *two*. It is possible for the answers for this section to overlap with the previous set of questions.

11 **seeing connections:** The answer is at the end of paragraph B: *Steve Jobs once said 'Creativity is about seeing connections'.*

12 **examine failure:** Question 10 should help you to locate the information in paragraph D: *Being able to examine failure, and analyse, tolerate and use it is an important part of both self-motivation and perseverance.* The heading for the paragraph should also help you.

13 **good/positive mood:** See the last sentence of paragraph E.

PAGES 50–53
Academic Reading Passage 2

Further Practice and Guidance (page 53)

Questions 14–18: Summary completion (without a wordlist)

1

e: In some cases the answer in a summary (with or without wordlists) or a table may not be in the order that it occurs in the reading passage. This can cause a lot of problems if students are not aware of it.

2

It is important to predict possible answers. You may be able to provide general words like items/things, people, vegetables, gadgets, fruit, places and so on, or ideas that are synonyms of the answer. Even if your prediction is the opposite, it will help you notice the answer. Sometimes, it is not possible to predict, but the words in the summary help you to focus on the answer as is the case in Question 18.

3

14 one word
15 one or two words
16 one or two words
17 one or two words
18 difficult to predict

Questions 14–18

The summary relates to the first main paragraph.

Note that not all questions are equally difficult in the Reading component. The level of difficulty of questions is mixed throughout the Reading test, but the test gradually becomes more difficult. It is easier to see this progression in the Listening and Speaking tests.

14 **consumption:** A noun is required here. The relevant sentence is: *The facts about children's digital consumption are eye-opening.* It is important not to repeat the word *digital* in the answer.

15 **electronic device:** The answer comes after the name of the study quoted in the third sentence: *using a smartphone, computer, television or other electronic device.* A summary does not always paraphrase the text completely as often words are used from the reading passage.

16 **children's media:** The answer comes just after the name of the second study: *Joan Ganz Cooney Centre, which specializes in children's media.*

17 **family member:** The answer is in the next sentence in the paragraph: *The Centre's own research suggests that most of the smartphones used by kids had been lent to them by a family member.*

18 **pass-back effect:** The answer is in the last sentence of the paragraph. Note the paraphrase: *aptly named the* (*a name that captures well the*). Note that the word *pass-back* has a hyphen and is one word. You may not fully understand the phrase, but this tests whether you understand the information around the phrase.

Questions 19–23

Note the rubric. Questions 19–23 are about the views of the writer.

19 **NOT GIVEN:** The second paragraph says: *A mere 20 years after the internet was founded, people do not yet know how the explosion in digital connectivity is shaping society.* The writer does not indicate any opinion about this. So we don't know if he/she thinks it is (*deeply*) worrying.

20 **YES:** In the same paragraph the writer says: *has both been called a benefit and curse for society. Looking back in history, the benefits of all these technologies have outweighed the problems they have caused.* The first sentence doesn't compare the past and present, but the second sentence weighs up the benefits and problems and the benefits are greater (*mainly positive*).

21 **YES:** In the fourth sentence of the second paragraph, the writer makes a suggestion (*Could it be that …?/It is possible that …*) about digital overload and children's education. Also notice *Perhaps* at the top of page 51, second line.

22 **NO:** The opinion is in the words *should not*. It is easy to miss the word *not*. Compare the sixth sentence of the second paragraph: *But that doesn't mean digital addiction is an issue we can just dismiss.* So it should be *a cause for concern*.

23 **NOT GIVEN:** In the third paragraph, apps are mentioned, but the writer does not give any positive or other evaluation (*The quality of apps for children is improving rapidly*).

Questions 24–27

24 **South Korea:** Note that the answers overlap slightly with the previous set of questions. The answer is in the second paragraph: *South Korea, one of the most digitally advanced nations in the world.* The word nation indicates that a name is mentioned.

25 **warnings:** The answer is in the fourth paragraph: *Some companies already include warnings on their electronic games about … .*
The word *company* in the heading *How far does a company's responsibility go?* helps you to locate the information.

26 **(a) dialogue:** Towards the end of the fifth paragraph, the writer says: *… the responsibility of the parent, who should have a dialogue.* The key word to look for is *parents* and some kind of suggestion (*should*).

27 **(their) privacy:** The key word to look for is (*the*) UK in the second from last paragraph and something to do with *safe* (*safety, protecting*): *lessons in internet safety and protecting their privacy.*

PAGES 54–56
Academic Reading Passage 3

Questions 28–34

The sentence beginnings to Questions 28–34 hold the key words to help you locate the information. The information in 28–34 is in the order it is in the passage. A–I are jumbled. The technique here is to read through the sentence beginnings and locate important information, e.g. *Roman.* Then read through A–I before looking at the reading passage.

Reading tasks like this can be time-consuming, but not if they are approached efficiently. An efficient technique here is to put a box around all the names relating to the bridges in the text. This helps to focus on the information about the bridges.

28 **D:** This is the first question so the answer is likely to be at the beginning. The answer is in the second paragraph: *It was not until the Romans introduced the arch that …*

29 **H:** Once Darby's bridge is located at the end of the second paragraph, the special information about it is clear: *Darby's Iron Bridge … well known for being the first of its kind in the world.*

30 **G:** The answer is at the end of the second sentence of the third paragraph: *… and intricate engravings.*

31 **A:** The answer is in the third sentence of the fourth paragraph: *a footbridge spanning an inlet.*

32 **B:** The answer is in the fifth paragraph: *before it was demolished and a fairly conventional five-arch stone bridge ... put in its place.* It is important not to confuse this with Tower Bridge in London.

33 **E:** The answer is at the end of the fifth paragraph: *Another famous bridge with commercial units still along its length today is the Ponte Vecchio across the River Arno.* Note the present tense in the sentence with *still* and *today* in the reading passage.

34 **I:** The answer is at the beginning of the sixth paragraph: *Many other bridges around the world have become instantly recognizable constructions.*

Questions 35–40

All of the information needed to complete the flow chart is in the sixth paragraph.

The technique here is to read the title and read through the flow chart looking for key words to help you look for information in the text. It is also useful to think about the kind of word (a noun, verb or adverb) that is required and to remember the word limit so extra words are not added. The heading for the flow chart helps to locate the information.

35 **army:** The information follows the design competition and relates to the building of the bridge: *an army of over 400 construction workers.* Note a noun beginning with a vowel is required and not a number.

36 **piers:** The answer is in the fifth sentence of the sixth paragraph: *construction of the bridge's famous towers and the walkways between them was supported by two immense piers.* It is important to remember not to put the word *immense* into the answer as only one word is allowed and also the adjective *huge* is already given in the question.

37 **bed:** The answer is immediately after the previous answer: *immense piers that were sunk into the river bed.* The clue is in the word *river*, which must not be written on the answer sheet.

38 **framework:** The word *steel* helps you to locate the answer, but comes after *framework* in the reading passage: *The framework ... employed more than 11,000 tons of steel.*

39 **appearance:** This word is located in the penultimate sentence of the paragraph: *The steel framework itself was then protected by covering it in Cornish granite and Portland stone, which also enhanced its appearance.* Note the paraphrasing using different structures and words: *protected* (*protecting*), *covering* (*encased in*), *enhanced* (*improving*).

40 **86:** Note the rubric, which allows a number. The answer is in the last sentence of the paragraph. Note the paraphrasing.

PAGES 57–59
Academic Writing Task 1

Possible answers

Version 1

Further Practice and Guidance (pages 58–59)

1

a Green space: *Green space was stated as very important by the vast majority of people in England in 2009.*

b A large proportion/Almost three-quarters: *A large proportion/Almost three-quarters of people in England stated that green space was very important.*

c 74%: *Seventy-four per cent/74% of people in England stated green space was very important.*

d 74%/a large proportion/almost three-quarters: *Those who thought green space was very important accounted for 74%/ a large proportion/almost three-quarters of the total.*

e Yes: *The overwhelming majority of people thought green space was very important.*

f *People rated the importance of green space very highly.*

g Positive: *People's attitude to green space was very positive.*

2

a state: *Green space was stated as ...*

b account for: *Those who thought ... accounted for 74% ...*

c the majority of: *The overwhelming majority of ...*

d think: *Those who thought ...*

e rate the importance of: *People rated the importance of ...*

3 Possible answers:

1 Green space was stated as fairly important by a minority of people in England in 2009.

2 A sizeable/significant proportion of people in England stated that green space was fairly important.

3 Twenty-one per cent/21% of people in England stated green space was fairly important.

4 Those who thought green space was fairly important accounted for 21%/just over a fifth of the total.

5 Some people/Just over a fifth of the total rated the importance of green space fairly highly.

6 Some people's attitude to green space was fairly positive.

4

a A sizeable *proportion* of *respondents* (28%) *gave* wanting to relax and unwind *as* a motivating *factor.*

b *Twenty-eight per cent* cited wanting to relax and unwind as *a factor* in *using* the natural environment.

c *Wanting to relax and unwind* was stated *by 28%* of respondents as a factor *for visiting* the natural environment.

d Wanting to relax and unwind *accounted for a significant proportion* (28%) of those *who visited the natural environment.*

e *Just over a quarter of respondents* (28%) *gave* wanting to relax and unwind *as a motivating factor.*

5

a More than half of visits (53%) were made to the countryside.

b Green space in towns and cities accounted for more than a third (37%) of visits.

c Seaside resorts or towns constituted 7% of visits compared to only 4% for other seaside coastline.

6

a More than half of visits (53%) were made to the countryside *compared to* more than a third (37%) to green space in towns and cities.

b *Although* more than half of visits (53%) were made to the countryside, green space in towns and cities accounted for more than a third (37%) of visits.

c *While* seaside resorts or towns constituted 7% of visits, only 4% was made to other seaside coastline.

7

a pie chart 2

b the overview for both pie charts

c pie chart 1

> *The pie charts show how important green space was to people in England in 2009 and the number of visits to the natural environment in 2009–11.*
>
> *Overall, it is clear that green space is seen by most people as fairly or very important with visits to green spaces in towns and cities accounting for a sizeable proportion of the total. For example, an overwhelming majority of people (74%) rated green space as being very important, followed by those rating it as fairly important accounting for 21%. Those rating green space as not very important made up only 4% of the total, while a small proportion (1%) said it was not important at all.*
>
> *The popularity of green space is shown by the volume of visits to green spaces in towns and cities in the second chart. Such trips made up 37% in both years out of a total of 2.49 billion compared to 53% for countryside visits. Seaside resort or town trips comprised 7% of the total, while other seaside coastline visits accounted for only a small proportion (4%).*

Word count: 179 words

Comments

The answer is more than 150 words and summarizes the information rather than listing it, e.g. the overview in the first sentence of the second paragraph (*Overall, it is clear …*) and the sentence at the beginning of the third paragraph (*The popularity of green space is shown by the volume of visits to green spaces in towns and cities in the second chart.*). There are complex sentences (*Those rating green spaces as not very important made up only 4% of the total, while*) and all the data is included. There is a wide range of grammatical structures and vocabulary (*is seen by, with visits to … accounting for a sizeable proportion of the total, compared to 53% for countryside visits*).

Version 2

Word count: 156 words

Comments

> *The charts below show the importance of green space to people in England in 2009 and the volume of visits to the natural environment in 2009-10 and 2010-11 in England.*
>
> *Green space is seen by the vast majority of people as fairly or very important. For example, a majority of people (74%) rated green space as being very important. This was followed by those rating it as fairly important. Those rating green space as not very important were only 4% of the total. A small proportion (1%) said they were not important at all.*
>
> *The popularity of green space is shown in the second pie chart. Out of a total of 2.49 billion visits to the natural environment in 2009-10 and 2010-11, visits to green space made up 37% of visits compared to 53% countryside visits. Visits to seaside or town were 7% of the total. Other seaside coastline visits were only a small proportion (4%).*

The introduction copies the rubric (note the inclusion of the word *below*), which might affect the overall score. The overview is not complete. The verbs *rate* and *to be* are repeated: common verbs describing data would be expected (*account for, constitute, make up, comprise*, etc). Note the repetition of the word *visits* in the third paragraph. There is little attempt at combining the information using complex sentences.

Use the Checklist on page 32 to help you assess your own answer and the possible answers.

PAGES 60–62
Academic Writing Task 2

Possible answers

Version 1

Further Practice and Guidance (pages 61–62)

Topic analysis
1 a development/trend: *is becoming more and more*
2 Yes: *Some people think …*
3 b

Collecting ideas
Technique 1
a technological – *convenience, quick, time-saving*; employment – (*negative*) *impact on job numbers*; health – *a sedentary lifestyle*; economic/financial – *closure of shops, reduced employment, lower tax revenue*; social – *reduced contact with people in shops*; age (young/elderly) – *pleasure for young people, difficulty for old people*
b personal, familial, local, regional, national, international/global

Technique 2
technological – *inconvenient, breaks down*; employment – *positive impact on job numbers, creates jobs*; health – *saves time for other activities*; economic/financial – *creation of new businesses, increased employment, higher tax revenue*; social – *increased contact with people, other activities*; age (young/elderly) – *pleasure for young and for old people*

Technique 3
Possible answer:
cheap: cheapness of online shopping
time: more time for other activities
harmful: harm to jobs
freedom: freedom to do shopping at any time
health: unhealthy lifestyle

Planning your essay
1 yes
2 yes
3 yes

Word count: 268 words

Comments

> *The popularity of online shopping is increasing all around the world. To some, this trend is affecting society in a negative way, but I feel that the positive effect is greater than the negative.*
>
> *It is understandable that some people feel online shopping is detrimental to society, because it is destroying town centres and people's jobs. Bookshops on many high streets in the UK, for example, have closed as people buy books online. Purchases of music and films on the internet have had a similar effect, leading to empty shops in high streets and the loss of local jobs. The same situation is prevalent in other countries around the world.*

I personally feel, however, that shopping online has an important role to play in modern life. Such shopping is not only convenient for shoppers, but it also creates jobs as internet businesses need to employ people. Further, over time the empty high street shops are gradually being replaced with other shops, which has always been the case. So, the impact on employment is probably, on balance, positive.

Another reason why online shopping is beneficial is the freedom it gives to people to do shopping at any time. This then provides people with time to do other activities such as sport or going out with the family. Moreover, it allows older people or housebound people of any age the opportunity to purchase goods, which they might not have the opportunity to do otherwise.

In conclusion, as with all new developments there are always going to be negative consequences, but, overall, I think the impact of online shopping is positive.

The answer is above 250 words. The answer is well organized with an introduction that paraphrases the rubric, topic sentences showing the content of each paragraph, and a suitable conclusion. The answer contains reasons (*because it is destroying town centres and people's jobs*) and examples (*Bookshops on many high streets in the UK, for example*), and has a range of grammatical structures and vocabulary (*Purchases of music and films on the internet have had a similar effect, leading to, The same situation is prevalent in other countries around the world*). There are no grammatical mistakes.

Version 2

In many countries around the world, online shopping is becoming more and more popular. Some people think that this is having a negative impact on society, but I feel that the positive impact is greater than the negative impact.

Some people think that this is having a negative impact on society, because it is destroying town centres and people's jobs. Bookshops have closed as people buy books online. Purchases of music and films on the internet have had an effect. This is leading to empty shops and the loss of jobs. The same situation is prevalent in other countries around the world.

I personally feel, however, that shopping online has an important role to play in modern life. Such shopping is not only convenient for shoppers. It also creates jobs. Also, over time the empty high street shops are gradually being replaced with other shops. This has always been the case. So, the impact on employment is probably positive, I think.

Another reason why online shopping is beneficial is the freedom it gives to people to do shopping at any time. This then gives people time to do other activities. Moreover, it allows older people or housebound people of any age the opportunity to purchase goods at any time they want. They might not have the opportunity to do so if it were not for online shopping.

In conclusion, as with all new developments there are always going to be negative consequences, but, overall, I think the impact of online shopping is positive.

Word count: 253 words

Comments

The introduction copies the rubric, which may affect the score.

Note also the repetition of *Some people think that this is having a negative impact on society* at the beginning of the second paragraph. The basic overall structure is fine and the question answers the task, but the ideas are not connected together using complex sentences so there is a limited range of structures. There are few examples and reasons.

PAGES 63–64
Speaking Part 2

Further Practice and Guidance (page 64)

a *I'm going to describe a place that …*
b *… when I was in my first year …*
c *… monthly …*
d *There are many reasons why I first went there, …*
e *… I think it was mainly because …*
f *… it gave me an opportunity to …*
g *… that also attracted me to …*
h *… it was always worthwhile.*
i *… it was a very valuable experience.*

PAGES 63–65
Speaking Part 3

Further Practice and Guidance (page 65)

Ways to begin
1
1 b, c
2 b, c
3 a, c

2
Phrases such as: *I think so, …; Yes, in my opinion it is, …; I suppose mainly …; I think …; In my case …; From my own point of view, …; I'd say yes, it ought to be.; …, but to me …*

Adjectives such as: *(very) popular/enjoyable/relaxing/important*

When you express opinions, you can use adjectives that evaluate something: *important, enjoyable* and use comparisons: *is better than, is more important than.*

You can use modal verbs (*should*) and if you are uncertain: *It depends, It is possible, It is probable, might, may.*

If you are certain, you can use *definitely.*

Compare **Yes/No/Not Given** statements in the Reading component.

Other phrases for *I think*: *I imagine, As far as I'm concerned, To my mind, It seems (that)*

TEST 3

PAGES 66–67
Listening Section 1

Questions 1–6

1 **B:** The student says she wants to store books: *it's books … about 60, I guess … clothes from the wardrobe …* She doesn't say she wants to store the wardrobe. So A is incorrect. C is incorrect because pictures are not mentioned.

2 **B:** The student says that: *there's a sofa, two chairs and a desk* she wants to store and then she says: The *rest of the furniture belongs to my landlord*. So A and C are incorrect.

3 **C:** The student says: *I'm taking anything breakable home with me.* So A and B are incorrect.

4 **C:** The cost is £15 per week plus the cost of the boxes – £1 each. She needs 15 boxes.

5 **B:** The man says the boxes will be *put together and wrapped in plastic*, so A is incorrect. C is incorrect as Marina will get a reference number for all of the storage. The answer is B as the boxes will be *put with the furniture in the storage unit*.

6 **A:** Today is Monday. The collection is on a Thursday, and Marina chooses the morning.

Questions 7–10

7 **Beech:** It is important to be careful about double letters.

8 **NW3 0SR:** The road and the town are given in the table, so you should be listening for a postcode. The student says *postcode* so you should expect to hear a combination of letters and numbers.

9 **June 14th:** From the table you can tell that a month and date will be given. The box for the collection date is completed with this type of information.

10 **726394IK:** You know when you hear *booking reference* that the answer is next.

PAGES 68–70
Listening Section 2

Further Practice and Guidance (pages 69–70)

Questions 11–13 and 17–20: Predicting answers

11 a noun b a month or year
12 a verb (-*ing*) b changing, improving
13 a noun b accountant, engineer

17 a noun – plural or uncountable   b meetings, trips, welfare
18 a noun – plural or uncountable   b progress, finances, upkeep
19 a noun   b team, group
20 a collective noun   b group

Questions 14–16: Selecting items

c The key word is 'new'. This is the limiting word in the question. You should be prepared to avoid the pitfall of making a selection that does not fit the full description.

Questions 11–13

11 **March:** It is September now.
12 **painting:** The *original plan* and *renovate* are key words here: *We were initially planning just to renovate the centre by doing some painting …*
13 **architect:** The answer must begin with a vowel because of *an*. In the recording, the speaker says *hired* which is a synonym for *employed*.

Questions 14–16

A, C, G in any order.

The speaker says that vending machines were an idea, but they opened a café instead. Similarly, they were going to have a large room for computers, but decided not to. E and F are not mentioned.

Questions 17–20

17 **events:** In the recording, it says *events for young people*, but no more than two words can be used.
18 **(smooth) running:** It is important to listen for the name of the person, which comes before a description of their duties.
19 **volunteer:** The words *the other permanent post* tells you that you are about to hear about the third staff member. The word *Post* is in the table, so you know the answer is about to be given.
20 **team:** After Martin's job title has been given, you can anticipate that his duties will be next.

PAGES 71–73
Listening Section 3

Further Practice and Guidance (page 73)

Questions 25–30: Completing a flow chart

1 It gives the subject/topic of the flow chart.
2 They tell you what each subsection is going to be about.
3 to check if you can process information in stages/steps
4 in note form
5 yes
6 Yes: from both the grammar and the context.

Questions 21–24

21 **B:** Erica says *The policy document of the bank describes them* (workers) *as an invaluable asset*, which is a paraphrase of *employees … an essential part of the business*.
22 **A:** Erica says that *employees are encouraged to take an active and regular role in the day-to-day running*. In other words, employees are invited to get involved in how the bank functions.
23 **C:** Mark says that he thinks Erica's placement is *enjoyable and rewarding*. He does not say anything about making contacts or it being challenging.
24 **C:** Erica believes that the bank's working practices *result in real benefits for the customers and clients of the bank*.

Questions 25–30

25 **systems, procedures** in either order: Both words are required for one mark. The key word to listen out for is *updates*.
26 **feedback:** A noun is required here. It is important to listen for the words *good chance* and *exchange*, or a synonym.
27 **line managers:** The key phrase to listen for is *Three-monthly* or a synonym (*every three months*) followed by *informal interviews*. The speaker says *an informal interview with staff is arranged with line managers*. Note that *staff* cannot be the answer as it is already in the flow chart.

28 personal development: The words to listen for are *they focus on improving* (*enhancing*). The word *your* is not necessary as the flow chart is in note form.

29 cash payment: A noun phrase is required. The key words are: *Yearly* and *Bonus scheme*. The speaker says *there's a bonus scheme … top achievers get a cash payment, and five extra days' holiday*.

30 achievements, goals in either order: Both words are required for one mark. The key words to listen out for here are the heading, *official appraisal system, detailed* (*in-depth*) and *everyone's* (*individual's* in the script).

PAGES 74–75
Listening Section 4

Questions 31–34

31 C: The answer is the phrase *In the past, the focus of responsible tourism was the Earth.* A is the present focus and B is incorrect.

32 B: The Maasai *have a fair say in tourism.* A is incorrect as they get some money from the profits, not all. C is incorrect as a focus on game reserves is not mentioned.

33 B: There are different zones for diving and fishing: *tour operators have played an important role by developing different zones for diving and fishing.* A is therefore incorrect. C is incorrect, as it doesn't say that tour operators benefit from this development. They helped to arrange it.

34 C: The key phrase in the recording is *connections with local people,* so visitors can learn about traditions, etc. A is what some visitors do, not what they should do. B is not what visitors should do to help preserve heritage, but what responsible tourism provides.

Questions 35–40

The answers in this type of question will usually be in order, so it is important to listen for the phrase or information that precedes the answer. Note that some of the lines in the notes do not have a space for the answer, so these should be used to make sure the right section is being looked at and to prepare to listen for the next answer.

35 travel articles: The speaker says *we can find out about the destination we're visiting* so you should be prepared for the answer. You also know that at least two things will be mentioned, one being *guidebooks*.

36 clothes: The speaker says *we need to think … about the clothes we pack* and *warm welcome if we're dressed appropriately*.

37 imported goods: Note the negative in this line of the notes.

38 endangered species: *what we mustn't do is buy products made from* is paraphrased in the question *Avoidance of purchases made from*.

39 improvements: A noun is required. Listen for the key words *return, tour operators, comments* (*feedback*) and *enjoyment* (*enjoyed*).

40 (tourism) blogs: The speaker says *It is also possible to actively participate in*, which is changed into a noun phrase in the notes. The key word to listen for is *participate*.

PAGES 76–80
Academic Reading Passage 1

Further Practice and Guidance (page 80)

Questions 4–7: Classification

1

1 **B:** *hit agriculture*, paragraph 2
2 **B:** an *empire collapsed*, paragraph 3
3 **A:** *steep increase in greenhouse gases*, paragraph 4

4 **B:** *a shift in the … winds*, paragraph 2
5 **B:** *colder temperatures*, paragraph 2

2

1 **B:** *the sea level rises, inundating settlements*, paragraph 5
2 **A:** *migrants from … northern cities*, paragraph 3
3 **C:** *threaten rural incomes*, paragraph 5
4 **B:** *contaminating fresh water*, paragraph 5

3

1 **B:** *hinder efforts to … combat malnourishment*, paragraph 5
2 **A:** *hit agriculture*, paragraph 2
3 **C:** *threaten … major food markets*, paragraph 5
4 **C:** *disappearance of the glaciers … which regulate river flow*, paragraph 5
5 **A:** *cities … were deserted*, paragraph 2; *migrants from … northern cities*, paragraph 3

Question 13: Global multiple-choice question

13

b, c, d, e, g, h

Questions 1–3

1 D: The answer is at the end of the first paragraph: *if we act now and act together*, and also *we must act together* in the previous sentence. A is incorrect as the passage says growth needs to *produce fewer greenhouse gases*, not that growth needs to be reduced. B is incorrect as there is no mention of countries making new decisions on how they develop, and C is mentioned but not linked to the control of climate change.

2 A: The answer is at the start of the second paragraph: *lower rainfall and colder temperatures*. B is incorrect as it was not the pyramids themselves which were brought down, but Egypt's kingdom. C is incorrect as the cities became deserted. D is incorrect as the opposite is true.

3 C: The answer is in the third paragraph, as without the grain the empire collapsed. A and B are mentioned, but are not the cause of the collapse. D is incorrect as the number of migrant workers is not mentioned.

Questions 4–7

All the answers are in the fifth paragraph.

4 C: The key phrase is: *hinder efforts to … combat malnourishment*.
5 B: The key phrase is: *The hastening disappearance of the glaciers*.
6 A: The key phrase is: *as the sea level rises, inundating settlements*.
7 B: The key phrase is: *will threaten rural incomes*.

Questions 8–12

The answers to the summary are in the last four paragraphs of the passage. Note: in each case, a noun is required and all the answers are plural nouns.

8 E: The answer is a synonym of *effects* in the third sentence of the sixth paragraph. Note also the paraphrasing of other vocabulary items: *catastrophic* (*disastrous*) and *irreversible* (*impossible to reverse*). C is incorrect as it is untrue. It is the results, not the causes of climate change, which are mentioned here.

9 B: The answer is in the third sentence of the eighth paragraph. H is incorrect as although the *cutting of emissions* may result in a cut in the *benefits of carbon-intensive development*, this is not stated. D is incorrect as it is not possible to reduce priorities. The implication is that high-income countries should change their priorities.

10 F: The answer is a synonym of *growth* in the eighth paragraph. The phrase *They also need to* is paraphrased in the summary as *simultaneously*, and introduces what else wealthy nations need to do. J is incorrect as it does not fit with the phrase *non carbon-intensive*.

11 **G:** The answer can be found in the last paragraph, and is a paraphrase of *opportunities* in the first sentence. A is incorrect as it is dealing with the situation that is a challenge, not what people are given.

12 **I:** The answer is a synonym of *problems* referred to (*them*) in the last sentence of the passage. Note that the information in the summary may not always be in exactly the same order as the passage, as is the case here. D is incorrect as climate change is a priority for the world to tackle.

Question 13

C: The overall purpose is to argue for the prevention of climate change. A is incorrect as the comparisons of the past with the present are used as examples to demonstrate the argument detailed in C. B is incorrect as the writer describes possible actions for prevention. D is incorrect as the writer is warning rather than reassuring people about the future of development.

PAGES 81–85
Academic Reading Passage 2

Further Practice and Guidance (pages 84–85)

Questions 14–18: Matching statements to people

1

A Pete Basiliere
1 the second paragraph
2 **a** no **b** yes **c** no **d** no
3 yes
4 no

B Jonathan Rowley
1 three: the third, fourth and ninth paragraphs
2 the process of creating 3D sunglasses
3 **a** no **b** no **c** yes **d** no
4 yes
5 He is unsure about it, and doesn't think it will take off.

C Olaf Diegel
1 the sixth paragraph
2 **a** no **b** no **c** yes **d** no
3 the future
4 It will develop.

D James McBennett
1 the seventh paragraph
2 **a** yes **b** no **c** no **d** no
3 *making the computer files that control 3D printers available to everyone*

E Dan Crow
1 the eighth paragraph
2 **a** no **b** no **c** no **d** yes
3 a movement *away from mass production*

2

14 He believes that access to design data will expand the use of 3D printing.
15 He realizes that a common belief about 3D printing is untrue.
16 He predicts that 3D printing will become more common in the home.
17 He does not believe domestic 3D printing will become widespread.
18 He sees 3D printing as part of an historical process.

Questions 14–18

14 **D:** The answer is in the seventh paragraph. The key phrase is: *making the computer files that control 3D printers available to everyone.*

15 **A:** The answer is in the second paragraph. The key phrase is: *many people think the technology is some years away, when it is available now.*

16 **C:** The answer is in the sixth paragraph. The key phrase is: *I believe that we will start to see home ownership appearing.*

17 **B:** The answer is in the last paragraph. The key phrase is: *is dismissive of the idea that home 3D printing will ever really take off.*

18 **E:** The answer is in the eighth paragraph. The key is the description he gives, starting with the Industrial Revolution and ending with the Digitization Revolution.

Questions 19–22

The diagram is based on the description of the process in the fourth paragraph.

19 **basin:** The diagram shows a 30 cm-deep container. The name of the container is given in the first sentence of the paragraph.

20 **laser:** The answer is given in the second sentence: *Heat is then applied by a laser 3,000 times.*

21 **points:** The key word here is the adjective *predefined* in the second sentence of the paragraph: *to predefined points over a layer just 0.1 mm deep, melting and fusing the powder.*

22 **designer:** The answer is in the fifth sentence of the paragraph. Note that £425 is not possible here as the rubric states *ONE WORD*, not a number.

Questions 23–26

23 **making prototypes:** The answer is in the first paragraph. A maximum of three words is required, so you cannot add *aerospace and automotive companies*. The phrase *replacements for bones* would be incorrect as this was *more recently*, whereas the question asks about the sector in which 3D printing began.

24 **no assembly required:** The answer is at the end of the third paragraph. The paragraph describes how the glasses are made, ending with what makes them unique.

25 **(many) web-based developments:** The answer is at the end of the fifth paragraph. Note that hyphenated words count as one word, so you could add *many*. *3D printing* is incorrect here, as it is mentioned in the question.

26 **(traditional) manufacturing methods:** The answer is at the end of the last paragraph. A noun phrase is needed here.

PAGES 86–89
Academic Reading Passage 3

Questions 27–32

27 **v:** The paragraph talks about things people believe, but are not fact. Heading **viii** is incorrect as it is the people who will be surprised, not the country that is surprising.

28 **i:** The paragraph focuses on the steps the family took to get information about tea-growing. Heading **ii** is incorrect, as the origins are mentioned only briefly at the beginning of the paragraph.

29 **vi:** The paragraph describes the harvesting of the first commercial crop which was then sold.

30 **ix:** The focus in the paragraph is on the various aspects of the natural environment (no insects and pests), animals that love the tender leaves, but stop when the bushes reach a certain age; organic working methods working towards producing leaves with quality and flavour.

31 vii: The paragraph describes what the project does in addition to manufacturing.

32 iii: The paragraph describes plans for future developments. Heading **iv** is incorrect as it is only one aspect of the paragraph.

Questions 33–37

33 FALSE: The information in paragraph A indicates the opposite: *There are comments that are not unknown, such as: 'I always buy Yorkshire tea. It's so good to think of it growing out there on the moors.'* Note the double negative *not unknown*.

34 TRUE: The answer is at the end of paragraph A. The key phrase is: *not so different from*, i.e. *similar to*.

35 FALSE: The answer is in the second sentence of paragraph B: *Of all the large estates ... this is the largest*, i.e. Tregothnan Estate.

36 TRUE: The information is in paragraphs B and C: *By 1999, ... the first plantings were made*, and *In spring 2005 ... first commercial crop ... plucked.*

37 NOT GIVEN: The answer is at the end of paragraph C. The tea went on sale, but no mention is made of whether it <u>all</u> sold. It is important to notice 'limiting' terms such as *all/every/ no/none*.

Questions 38–40

38 more resistant: The answer is in the second sentence of paragraph D, but it is necessary to refer back to the first sentence to find out what *they* (the tea bushes) and *these animals* (rabbits, etc) refer to: *they are more resistant to these animals.*

39 quality and flavour: The information is at the end of paragraph D.

40 sells (baby/tea) bushes: In paragraph E *Alongside* is a synonym for *In addition to*. It is important to keep to the word limit. The text says *sells baby tea bushes*, which would be too many words.

PAGES 90–92
Academic Writing Task 1

Further Practice and Guidance (pages 91–92)

1

To describe something that is no longer there	To describe something that changed	To describe something that is new
demolish	renovate	add
pull down	improve	erect
replace	develop	build
knock down	extend	construct
make way for	turn into	create
remove	modernize	
give way to	convert into	

2

a A derelict building *was demolished/was pulled down/was replaced (by) .../was knocked down/made way for .../was removed/gave way to ...*

b An old-fashioned hotel *was renovated/was improved/was developed/was extended/was turned into .../was modernized/ was converted (into ...)*

c A modern leisure centre *was added/was erected/was built/ was constructed/was created*

3

Something that is no longer there	Something that changed	Something that is new
woodland	motel	golf course
farmland	garages	swimming pool and spa
	tearooms	airport
	woodland	marina

4

a The marina is *south of/to the south of* the village.

b The swimming pool and spa are *north of/to the north of* the village.

c The airport is *east of/to the east of* the village.

d The seafood restaurant is *west of/to the west of* the village.

e The hotel complex is *north-west of/to the north-west of* the village.

Possible answers

Version 1

The maps show the coastal region of Melvin Island at two different times, 2000 and 2010. It is clear that between the two dates a number of significant changes were made to the area.

Looking at the first map, it can be seen that the coastal area was largely undeveloped, with a village surrounded by woodland and farmland. There were only two facilities for visitors: a motel to the north and tearooms to the west of the village. To turn to the second map, it is clear that many developments took place. The motel was turned into a hotel complex, while the adjacent garages were demolished and the chalets erected in their place. The tearooms were knocked down and replaced by a seafood restaurant with the woodland to the north of the village giving way to a golf course.

In addition, several new amenities were constructed. A swimming pool and spa were built to the north of the village, and a marina and airport were created.

Word count: 167 words

Comments

The answer is well constructed, with a clear introduction and overview. The main changes have been fully described, with a good range of structures and vocabulary. The passive is used effectively, as is a range of connectors.

Version 2

In the maps we can see how part of an island looked at two dates. It is clear that quite a few changes happened between the times.

In the first map, we can see that there was not much on the coast, only a village with some woods and farmland. Visitors could only go to a motel or some tearooms. In the second map, a lot of things have changed. The motel has gone and there is a hotel there instead, and also the garages are not there anymore, but there are chalets instead. The tearooms are no longer there and there is a seafood restaurant. On one side of the village, there used to be some woodland, but now there is a golf course in its place.

Also, some new things were built. Now there is a swimming pool and a spa, and a marina and an airport as well.

Word count: 151 words

Comments

Most of the information is given and there is an overview. The introduction is not written in a formal style. There is a lot of repetition of vocabulary and structures (*we can see*, the verb *to be*, *there is*, *there was*) and the overall sentence structure is very similar (*The tearooms are no longer there and there is a seafood restaurant*; *Now there is a swimming pool and a spa*). There is little attempt to combine information.

PAGES 93–95
Academic Writing Task 2

Further Practice and Guidance (pages 94–95)

1
i d **ii** e **iii** b **iv** g **v** f **vi** a **vii** c

2
b Therefore/Because of this/As a result of this/Consequently
c are caused by/stem from/result from
d is an important factor in/is a significant factor in/has an influence on/has an impact on
e causes/leads to/gives rise to/results in
f Therefore/Because of this/As a result of this/Consequently
g The effect of … is/The consequence of … is

3
Possible causes: good work opportunities/migration
– *Good work opportunities have an indirect impact on the availability of cheap housing.*
– *A shortage of accommodation is caused by the migration of people to cities.*

Possible solutions: new housing, cheaper transport
– *More high-rise buildings such as skyscrapers could be built.*
– *The cost of transport could be made much cheaper.*

Possible answers

Version 1

Many large urban areas are facing increases in the cost of living, which means that soon only the wealthy will be able to afford to live and work there. There are many factors contributing to this situation, but several approaches could be adopted to tackle the problem.

One of the main reasons for the high cost of city living is that cities such as London attract people from other parts of the country as well as the world, because they offer a wider range of employment opportunities and high salaries. This then results in increased house prices and rents, as greater numbers of workers try to find somewhere to live.

Another factor is that cities generally have better facilities such as education, health and entertainment, which are more limited elsewhere. For example, the top schools and universities are often in major cities such as New York or Boston or San Francisco, which draws in people from other areas.

The main measure to remedy the above situation is to create more affordable housing. For example, more skyscrapers could be built within or on the edge of cities such as Paris or Berlin. Alternatively, creating new satellite towns in the areas surrounding a city would also be possible. Such developments would reduce the pressure on the cost of housing in cities and make accommodation affordable for everyone. Another strategy is to encourage people living in smaller cities, towns and villages to stay there by improving facilities and attractions.

As can be seen, there are a number of reasons why city life is expensive, but several steps can be taken to remedy the situation.

Word count: 271 words

Comments

The essay is well structured, with a clear introduction, two paragraphs describing the causes, and one paragraph suggesting measures which can be taken to resolve the problem, as well as a conclusion.

A wide range of vocabulary and structures is used (*urban areas, many factors contributing to, approaches, could be adopted to tackle, reasons, employment opportunities, draws, steps*). The body paragraphs are connected to the introduction and the task by the use of topic sentences at the beginning of the paragraphs. Reasons (*because they offer a wider range of employment opportunities and high salaries*) and examples (*For example, the top schools and universities*) are also given along with complex sentences (*There are many factors contributing to this situation, but several approaches could be adopted to tackle the problem.*). Each of the paragraphs is well constructed.

Version 2

Many large urban areas are facing increases in the cost of living. So soon only the wealthy will be able to afford to live and work there. There are many major reasons for this situation, but several measures could be taken to deal with the problem.

One of the main reasons for the high cost of city living is that cities attract people. They offer a wide range of employment opportunities and high wages. The result is increased house prices and rents, as increasing numbers of workers try to find somewhere to live.

Another reason is that cities often have better facilities, which are often more limited in other parts of the country. For example, the top schools and universities are often in major cities. This draws in people from other areas and from around the globe as both national and international migrants are drawn to these major cities.

The main measure to remedy the above situation is to create more affordable housing. More skyscrapers could be built within or on the edge of cities. Alternatively, creating new towns in the areas surrounding a city would also be possible. The developments would reduce the pressure on the cost of housing in cities and make accommodation affordable for everyone. Another measure is to encourage people living in smaller cities, towns and villages to stay there by improving facilities and attractions.

As can be seen, there are a number of reasons why city life is expensive, but several measures can clearly be taken to remedy the situation.

Word count: 255 words

Comments
The answer generally deals with the topic and there are topic
sentences connecting the body paragraphs to the introduction and
the task. However, in most cases the sentences just sit next to each
other without any attempt at connecting them (e.g. in the second
paragraph). Vocabulary is often repeated (*reason* and *measure*
throughout, and *often* in the third paragraph). There are few
examples and reasons which means that the explanations
throughout are not clear.

PAGES 96–97
Speaking Part 2

Further Practice and Guidance (page 97)

1 a, h   **2** b, e, g   **3** i   **4** c, d, f

PAGES 96–98
Speaking Part 3

Further Practice and Guidance (page 98)

Gaining experience
Work placements and volunteering
– *acquiring up-to-date ICT skills, internet use, social media use,
   global understanding, interpersonal skills*
What will happen if young people don't gain new knowledge
and experience/skills?
– *won't be able to fit in, will be disadvantaged in the workplace
   and will be left behind or excluded in many situations*
Use of technology in training, e.g. online tasks, simulation
– *language training, computer translation, e.g. mobile phones
   instant translation, robotic patients training doctors and
   nurses*

Importance of knowledge and experience

Experiences we have of being in a family, class or community
– *respect for others, sharing, patience, manners, discipline*
Knowledge gained by studying
– *basic reading and writing skills, more precise knowledge in
   various subjects*
Experience needed for the modern world
– *using computer/mobile phone skills, social media use,
   self-checkout in supermarkets, updating skills, working in
   teams, etc*
General experience vs specific skills
– *both important, both essential*

Test 4

PAGES 99–101
Listening Section 1

Further Practice and Guidance (page 101)

Questions 1–5: Multiple-choice questions

1 a historic sights
   b what's new
2 a royal attractions
   b no
   c Windsor Castle
3 a no
   b no
   c they are *great fun*
4 a It's got a very wide range of contemporary art from around the world.
   b Yes: *from around the world*
   c no
5 a experience a view of the whole city from above/get some great photos
   b if you book in advance/if there are enough of you

Questions 1–5

1 **A:** The speaker says *Mostly the historic sights*. B is incorrect as the speaker is also (but not more) interested in *what's new*. C is not mentioned.
2 **B:** The speaker has limited time, and Windsor Castle is *quite a way outside London*. A and C are not mentioned.
3 **C:** The woman says *Both have a lot of interactive exhibits, which makes them great fun*. A is incorrect as it is not mentioned, and B is what the speaker does not want.
4 **B:** The visitor says *I've heard it's got a very wide range of contemporary art from around the world*. A is incorrect as *British* is not mentioned. C is incorrect because *European* is not mentioned and the art is *from around the world*, not just Europe.
5 **B:** A private capsule is a good idea *if there are enough of you*. A is incorrect as the speaker says you have to book in advance, but *a week* is not mentioned, and C is not mentioned.

Questions 6–10

6 **relaxing:** An adjective is needed here. This is clear from the structure of this line of the notes.
7 **talks:** A noun is needed here. The words *in 10 languages* help you decide what kind of noun you will need.
8 **secret:** it is important to follow the notes about bicycle tours to listen for the missing information, which will come after a reference to being fit. An adjective is needed here.
9 **features:** a noun is needed here and *interactive* is the key word to listen for.
10 **21:** A number is needed here. Care must be taken not to be confused by the question number, which always goes before the space. Note the word *over* in the recording is paraphrased by *or more* after the blank space, so it cannot be added on the answer sheet.

PAGE 102
Listening Section 2

Questions 11–14

11 **D:** The speaker says the canopy *needs a few minor repairs*.
12 **F:** The word *free* is paraphrased by the phrase *It won't cost us anything*. Note that the speaker also says *the venue's obviously free*, i.e. the school playing field, but this is not one of the items in the list.
13 **B:** The speaker says *All we'll need to do is pay for the insurance*. Note the paraphrase of *necessary*.
14 **E:** The speaker mentions the topic of food and drink, and then says *the school governors are likely to subsidize a barbecue, so it won't be expensive*. Even if you are not familiar with the meaning of *subsidize*, the second part of the sentence tells you the barbecue will not be expensive, i.e. *cheap*.

Questions 15–18

15 **clearly:** The key phrase to listen out for is *audience-free zone*, but this comes after the information you need for the answer. It is necessary to be able to process 'chunks' of language and process them to extract the answer. The speaker mentions the *safety aspect*, which helps you prepare for the answer.
16 **access:** The *three-hour set-up time* is mentioned, which helps you to prepare for the answer.
17 **power/electricity:** When the speaker mentions *the performance area* and the adjectives *suitable and safety-certificated*, the answer is about to be given. The speaker also mentions *electricity*, so this is also acceptable as a key.
18 **safety:** An adjective is needed here. Note that this question requires interpretation of what you hear, i.e. what the speaker is *sure (confident)* about.

Questions 19 and 20

19 **B:** The group advertise on their social media pages. A is incorrect as the group advertise on their website not the school's; C is incorrect as it is the speaker who mentions advertising in the local paper.
20 **C:** The speaker says *it would be a good idea if each class teacher organized a poster competition*. A is incorrect as free tickets are mentioned as prizes for the best entries; B is what the speaker will do himself, not the children.

PAGES 103–106
Listening Section 3

Further Practice and Guidance (pages 105–106)

Questions 21–27

1
All of the hints can help to 'trigger' the answer. While preparing for the IELTS test, it is important to think of different ways to trigger answers so that in the exam itself you are able to do it automatically.

2
a person: *persons, personality/personalities, personable, personalize, personalizes, personalized, personalization, impersonal*
b restriction: *restrict, restricts, restricted, restricting, restrictive, unrestricted*
c choose: *chooses, chosen, choosing, chose, choice*
d different: *difference, differ, differs, differed, differentiate, indifferent, indifference*
e expenditure: *expend, expended, expense, expensive, inexpensive*

Questions 21–23

The heading tells us that the answers are about an article that Sophie has chosen to comment on. Sophie may give the answers for all three questions, but note that the instruction at the beginning of the recording tells us that there are three speakers. The answers may come very closely to the beginning of the recording or be spread throughout.

Note the word limit. It is important to think of the type of word that is needed in each case. It is also important to predict the answers, e.g. Is the answer to 21 a verb (infinitive or -*ing* form) or a noun? Is the meaning positive (e.g. *increasing*) or negative (e.g. *decreasing*)?

21 restricting: A verb in the -*ing* form is needed here. The answer comes towards the beginning of the conversation. Brad asks Sophie and Miyaki if they have selected their article to comment on. The words to listen for when Sophie speaks are *gone for* (*chosen*) and *on* (*I've gone for this one on ... restricting government funding*).

22 angry: An adjective is needed here. Sophie gives her opinion of the article where she says ... *my immediate reaction is that it's effectively nonsense*. It is then Miyaki who says *The article seems to have made you quite angry*, and Sophie agrees. It is important not to add the word *quite* to the answer as this is in the test.

23 government attitudes: A noun phrase is needed here. The words to listen for are *articles like the one* Sophie *has chosen* or a paraphrase of *this* and *can affect* (*have an effect/impact on/have consequences for*, etc): *articles like this can have consequences for government attitudes to*. Note the word *attitudes* has to be in the plural form in this sentence.

Questions 24–27

The general comments at the beginning of the previous section also apply here.

24 personalities: A noun is needed here. Brad starts off by asking Sophie about her comments on the article (*So what are you going to say in your comments about the article?*). Sophie refers to the table (*I've got a rough table here on a piece of paper*) and then indicates she is going to mention the first point (*for a start*). Then the contradiction is mentioned ('*but*' *not everyone is suited to studying science, technology, ...*) and the reason is given (*because all of us have different goals and personalities*). Note the word *different* must not be included in the answer as the word limit is one word.

25 core: A noun/noun phrase is needed here. Sophie indicates that she is going to make the next point (*secondly*), which is summarized by the notes in the table. After the point is made, the answer is given when Sophie mentions her contradiction (*But these subjects are vital core subjects*), which she introduces again with the word *but*. The answer is given after the word *crucial* or a synonym (*vital, important, essential*, etc). Note: it is important not to include the word *vital* in the answer (the word limit is one word and the word *crucial* is already in the test).

26 pumped: A past participle is needed here. Sophie indicates her third point (*And thirdly*). The answer then comes once Sophie has introduced the point (*extra money should be given to students and universities that train scientists and engineers*). She indicates her contradiction this time using *however*.

27 expense: A noun is needed here. The answer comes immediately after Sophie's contradiction. This time she gives her reason by first agreeing, then contradicting: *We do need engineers, but not at the expense of other investment in other subject areas.*

Questions 28–30

C, F, G in any order.

The answers occur in the following order: C, G, F. Underline the nouns in the alternatives to help you identify the points. A is not correct as all the main points need to be included: *I should highlight the main points of the article ... Then in writing I restate the main points.* B is not mentioned and Miyaki says *restate ... with the main supporting evidence.* D and E are not mentioned.

PAGE 107

Listening Section 4

Questions 31–40

31 attachments: A noun is required. The heading indicates that this part of the recording relates to work. The key words to listen for are *benefited* (*all students on courses in the department have benefited*), before taking the course (*before joining the diploma course*), and *day-release work*.

32 practical: An adjective is required here. When you hear *Employers don't just want qualifications. This doesn't mean that qualifications aren't important, they are* you know you are about to hear the answer.

33 placed: An adjective or a past participle used as an adjective is required. The key words to listen for are *graduating* or synonyms (*leaving/finishing*) of this, and *diploma* (or *course*): *but all students finishing the course are very well placed as far as the job market is concerned.*

34 start-ups: A noun is required. When current or future domination global companies are mentioned, the key words are: *emphasis, small companies* and *tech*, or paraphrases of these words: *While the future world is likely to be more dominated by global enterprises, business people and governments are also likely to emphasize the need for more small companies, such as flexible tech start-ups.*

35 (changing) market trends: A noun/noun phrase is required. The key words are: *secret, company, dynamic, speedy reaction* or paraphrases of these words: *the secret is to develop an enterprise that is dynamic and can respond fast to changing market trends.*

36 contacts: A noun/noun phrase is required. The heading *Networking* is key to finding the answer. Other key words are *opportunities* and *make*. It is possible to predict the word *contacts* here.

37 challenges: A noun/noun phrase is required. The headings *Networking* and *'Going it alone'* are key here. It is important to process the notes carefully here; try to use prediction and collocation to help you. Possible words that you might have predicted here are words such as *difficulties, situations, obstacles* and *threats*. Note the spelling with double *l* and that only the plural is acceptable here.

38 reputation: A noun/noun phrase is required. The key words are: *economic potential, jobs, growth, benefit, local economy*, which you hear before ... *and incidentally the reputation of the university, especially this department.*

39 critical thinking: A noun/noun phrase is required. The key phrases are the headings *World skills module* and *Non-cognitive skills: non-cognitive skills have been the main focus. These have included opportunity recognition, innovation, critical thinking, resilience, decision-making ... .*

40 pilot scheme: A noun/noun phrase is required. Listen for *finance sourcing* and *setting up independent businesses* in the notes. The key words are: *in conjunction with* (simply *with* in the notes), *university* and *exciting new*: ... *even in conjunction with the university, including an exciting new pilot scheme ...*

PAGES 108–111
Academic Reading Passage 1

Further Practice and Guidance (page 111)

Questions 6–10: True/False/Not Given (Comparison and contrast)

1

1 f, g, j **2** a, h **3** c **4** b, d, k **5** e, i

2

Notice how negatives and adverbs can be used to express comparison. It is also important to notice which of the items/aspects being compared comes first in a sentence.

1 c, f

A is slightly (comparative) than B = B is not quite as (adjective) as A

A is slightly (comparative) than B = B is marginally (comparative) than A

2 b

A is nowhere nearly as (adjective) as B = B is much (comparative) than A

3 a, d

A is substantially (comparative) than B = B is much (comparative) than A

A is substantially (comparative) than B = B is a lot (comparative) than A

4 e

A is not quite as (adjective) as B = B is slightly (comparative) than A

Questions 1–5
B, D, F, G, I in any order.

B is mentioned in the first paragraph. D is mentioned in the first sentence of the second paragraph. F is mentioned in the first sentence of the third paragraph. G is mentioned at the end of the third paragraph. I is mentioned in the first sentence of the fourth paragraph.

A is incorrect as its *healing properties* are mentioned at the end of the first paragraph. C is incorrect as it says the plant *grows in subtropical climates* at the end of the second paragraph. E is incorrect as there is no mention of how long the flowers last. H is incorrect as it says *The roots contain the medicinally active constituents* in the second paragraph. J is incorrect as in the fourth paragraph it states that (*horizontal) runners ... throw up stems in their second year*.

Questions 6–10
6 FALSE: The answer is at the start of the fifth paragraph: *English-grown liquorice is dug up in late autumn and sold mostly in its fresh state for making extract, with only a small amount being dried.* This means all of it.
7 TRUE: The answer is in the last sentence of the fifth paragraph. English liquorice has *a more delicate flavour than that of imported varieties.*
8 FALSE: The opposite is true. The answer is at the end of the sixth paragraph: *this* (i.e. Spanish liquorice) *cultivation has grown rapidly.*
9 NOT GIVEN: In the seventh paragraph, it says that Russian liquorice has a bitter taste, but there is no mention of whether this affected its popularity.
10 FALSE: In the seventh paragraph, it says Russian liquorice has a different taste.

Questions 11–13
11 C: The answer is at the start of the ninth paragraph. B is incorrect as liquorice *will not flourish on clay.*
12 A: The answer is in the tenth paragraph: *cool weather interferes with the formation of ... juice.* D is incorrect as in the same paragraph it states that the plant can *not endure severe freezing.*
13 E: The answer is in the first sentence of the last paragraph.

PAGES 112–116
Academic Reading Passage 2

Further Practice and Guidance (page 116)

Questions 14–20: Matching headings
The statements help you to think about the whole section and not just focus on individual parts of the section or paragraph. For exam preparation purposes, it is possible to write several statements about paragraphs/sections to help analyse them. It is also useful to make questions to help you examine the paragraph, for example:

Section A
a Does the section introduce the topic of the article?
b Does it contain something that relates to 'beginning'?
c Is the section about a new idea?
d Is the idea international, not local?

Questions 14–20
14 iv: The section is about how the concept or idea of smart cities came about (*is a concept that has come into being in recent years; ... it has gained even greater prominence as ...*). Note that this section does not contain an explanation, so the answer is not **vii**. The concept is introduced first and then the explanation.
15 vii: The answer is in the first two sentences of the first paragraph in the section (*The concept of a smart city goes way beyond the transactional relationships ... It is essentially about*), and the first sentence of the second paragraph in the section (*there is no absolute definition of a smart city, no end point, but rather a process, or series of steps, by which ...*). Note the paragraph does not give criteria as to what makes a city smart, so the answer is not **i**. The answer is not **v** as this is only a detail or example of what makes up a smart city – see the last sentence of both paragraphs. Note that if all the information about attractiveness is removed, the section heading still works.
16 ii: The section contains examples of cities from different parts of the world that are possible competitors for the title of the top smart city.
17 i: The section is a list of the main features/characteristics/criteria for judging what a smart city is. Heading **ix** is not correct as it is a detail relating to the fifth criteria in the last sentence of the section.
18 vi: The first sentence indicates that the topic discussed in this section is in addition (*the sixth ... criterion*) to the criteria discussed in the previous section.
19 iii: The section is clearly about urbanization, not economic development, which comes in the next section. The answer cannot be **x** as this is only a detail and does not cover the whole section. The answer is not **viii** because it does not analyse economic growth in the present and future.
20 viii: This section is about economic development and covers the present and the future. It is not about the growth of urbanization, which is discussed in the previous section, so the answer cannot be **iii**.

Questions 21–25

A, B, C, F, G in any order.

The answers to this section are found in Section D. The order they occur in the text is F, A, C, G, B. Note the first sentence in Section D indicates that five items are discussed and the items are clearly marked (*The first, the second key aspect, The third aspect, Another, And lastly*). There is no mention of D, and E is a detail related to the second aspect, not an aspect in itself.

Question 26

C: A relates only to Section C, B relates to Section D only, and the only mention of D is in the last section.

PAGES 117–119
Academic Reading Passage 3

Questions 27–31

It is important to remember that a claim is a statement which someone says is true. The information may be given in the reading passage, but the writer may contradict it or not make a claim about it.

27 **YES:** The answer is in the penultimate sentence of the first paragraph: *The male of the Great Bird of Paradise with its vibrant colour and fluffy, scarlet feathers, is the most spectacular-looking member of this very flamboyant species.*

28 **NO:** In the first line of the second paragraph, the writer states: *This bird occurs on New Guinea and its surrounding islands.* So it is found in more than one place. Notice the use of the word *only* in the statement to 'limit the location' to one place.

29 **NOT GIVEN:** The answer is in the third and fourth lines of the third paragraph: *The black crow and the jay are, in fact, related to the bird of paradise. Some species are black and resemble the black crow, but most birds of paradise are brightly coloured with long tail feathers, making them look more like a peacock than a crow.* The writer states they are related, but no information is given about how close.

30 **YES:** The answer is in the last sentence of the third paragraph: *Female birds live in small groups, but the males are usually solitary.*

31 **NO:** The statement indicates that the writer made a claim about the purpose of the call of the male bird. In the first sentence of the fourth paragraph, the writer says what the purpose is: *In the mating season, the male makes a very peculiar and very loud call, the sole purpose of which is to lure the female.*

Questions 32–35

It is important to locate the information by scanning for the key words. Certain words may be repeated, and some names or dates may be given. Also think of synonyms of words and phrases in the sentences. As in other sets of questions it is useful to write the number of the answer of a question in the margin of the text. The answers are in order and so it helps you navigate or find your way around the text when you look for the other answers.

32 **significant:** An adjective is required. The answer is in the first line of the fifth paragraph: *The bird of paradise has a significant role in Papuan culture.*

33 **50,000:** A number is required. After scanning for the phrase *By the early 1900s* or a paraphrase (*by the beginning of the 20th century*) and a number, the answer is in the last sentence of the sixth paragraph. The answer should not include the word *about*, because the word *approximately* is in the sentence in the test.

34 **Metu Debi:** A name is required (see the word *location*). The phrase *around the very beginning of the 20th century* also helps to locate the information in the text. The answer is in the second sentence of the seventh paragraph.

35 **embargo:** A noun is required. Note the indefinite article *an*, which means that the word begins with a vowel. Care must be taken not to add the word *trade* here. The answer is in the first sentence of the last paragraph.

Questions 36–39

It is important to use the classification to help you navigate or find your way around the reading passage. The first step is to find out if the dates in A–C are limited to one part of the text, and then to put a box around each time date or reference to these centuries. It is useful to keep in mind that the 16th century is 1500–1599, the 19th century is 1800–1899 and the 20th century is 1900–1999.

36 **B:** The answer is in the fifth sentence of the sixth paragraph.

37 **C:** The answer is in the first sentence of the last paragraph.

38 **A:** The answer is in the second sentence of the sixth paragraph. The period is given at the end of the sentence.

39 **B:** The answer is in the seventh sentence of the sixth paragraph.

Question 40

B: The answer is in the last sentence of the text: *Today, the bird of paradise is still popular across the globe because of its beauty.* Also see the first sentence of the text: *The male bird of paradise with its strikingly colourful plumage is just as amazing a spectacle in the jungle of New Guinea today as it has always been.*

PAGES 120–122
Academic Writing Task 1

Further Practice and Guidance (pages 121–122)

1

a mostly man-made: the first stage is part of a natural process

b ten main phases/steps, with the last phase having three alternatives

c No: only as part of the introduction or overview – see Version 1 on page 152. The task is about the life cycle of a cotton T-shirt, of which the production process is part.

d points

e the passive

f mainly nouns

g to harvest, to transport, to spin, to weave, to design, to dye, to produce/to package, to sell, to wear, to throw away, to incinerate, to recycle

h mainly the present simple as it is a repeated process. The present perfect can be used when information is combined, e.g. *Once [the cotton] is/has been [picked], it is [sent]…*

i a selection of adverbs: *first/first of all, second/secondly, then, next, following that, afterwards, after that, subsequently, finally*

j a selection of conjunctions: *when, where, after, before, once, immediately, until*

2

1 The bushes produce cotton.

2 The cotton is harvested by the cotton picker.

3 The raw material is put into bales/is baled.

4 The bales are shipped (transported) to a factory.

5 The cotton is turned into woven cloth/is woven into cloth.

6 The T-shirt is designed.

3

a Once the bushes produce cotton, it is harvested by the cotton picker.

b Before the raw material is shipped (transported) to a factory/ Before being shipped (transported) to a factory, the raw material is put into bales/is baled.

c After the cotton is turned into woven cloth/is woven into cloth, the T-shirt is designed.

It is important to note the changes, once the information is turned into complex sentences.

4

The designing of the T-shirt/The design stage/phase.

The manufacture/manufacturing of the T-shirt/The manufacturing stage of the T-shirt.

The production/producing of the T-shirt/The production stage of the T-shirt.

The transport/transportation/transporting of the T-shirt/ finished product.

The sale/selling of the T-shirt.

The burning/incinerating of the T-shirt.

The recycling of the T-shirt/The recycling stage of the T-shirt.

Possible answers

Version 1

> *The diagrams illustrate the life cycle of a cotton T-shirt. It is clear that from the growth of the cotton to the throwing away, incinerating or recycling of the garment, there are multiple stages in its life cycle.*
>
> *First of all, the cotton bushes grow and produce cotton. At the harvesting stage, the cotton is picked by a machine called a cotton picker. Then the raw material is put into bales and transported to a factory where the cotton is spun into thread before being woven into cloth. Following the design stage, the finished cloth is sent to a manufacturer to be dyed and made into a T-shirt. Once it has been printed and dyed, it is packaged and sent to a shop where it is sold. The consumer wears the T-shirt until it becomes shabby, after which it is thrown away as rubbish, incinerated or recycled as industrial cloth or insulation material.*

Word count: 155 words

Comments

The introduction paraphrases the rubric (*The diagrams illustrate the life cycle of a cotton T-shirt*) and there is a clear overview in the second sentence. All of the information is included in the answer, and summarized using complex sentences, e.g. the third sentence of the second paragraph where four steps are combined together: *Then the raw material is put into bales and transported to … where the cotton … before being woven … .* The answer contains a range of adverbial phrases (*First of all* and *At the harvesting stage*) and conjunctions to make complex sentences: *a factory <u>where</u> the cotton, <u>Once</u> it, the T-shirt <u>until</u>, <u>after</u> which it.*

Version 2

> *The diagrams illustrate the life of a cotton T-shirt. It is clear that there is a series of steps involved in the life cycle. There is the growth of the cotton, the production process for the manufacturing of the T-shirt, and the throwing away, incinerating or recycling of the garment.*
>
> *The cotton bushes grow and produce cotton. The cotton is picked by a machine called a cotton picker. Then the raw material is put into bales and transported to a factory. In this factory, the cotton is spun into thread before it is woven into cloth. The design stage comes next and the cloth is sent to a manufacturer. It is dyed and made into a T-shirt. The T-shirt is then packaged and sent to a shop and it is sold. The consumer wears the T-shirt until it becomes shabby and after that it is thrown away as rubbish, incinerated or recycled as industrial cloth or insulation.*

Word count: 157 words

Comments

The introduction paraphrases the rubric (*The diagrams illustrate the life of a cotton T-shirt*), and there is an overview in the second and third sentences, which are not well connected. All of the information is included in the answer and there are no mistakes, but the stages of the process are not signalled well (*The design stage comes next and the cloth is sent to a manufacturer*), involve repetition (*and transported to a factory. In this factory*), and are sometimes just listed (*It is dyed and made into a T-shirt. The T-shirt is then packaged and sent to a shop and it is sold*). As a result of poor cohesion, the answer therefore lacks clarity.

PAGES 123–124
Academic Writing Task 2

Further Practice and Guidance (page 124)

1

a Yes: the present continuous tense *is being carried out.*

b advantages and disadvantages

c **Possible answers:**

advantages: *benefits, positive impact/effects/aspects, beneficial, has a positive impact/effect on*

disadvantages: *drawbacks, downsides, negative impact(s)/effect(s)/aspects, have a negative impact/effect on, harmful/detrimental*

d Yes: alternatively, the essay could be organized: introduction, two/three body paragraphs with the advantage(s) in one or two paragraph(s) and the disadvantage(s) in one or two paragraph(s) and conclusion.

e Yes: all are relevant.

Possible answers

Version 1

> *Machines are increasingly performing many tasks, both in the home and the workplace, that were previously done by humans. This phenomenon has brought many benefits, but there is no denying that there are many drawbacks.*
>
> *A major advantage is that domestic appliances such as dishwashers and washing machines, and now robotic vacuum cleaners have made people's lives more comfortable. For example, these devices have given people more freedom by allowing them more time to devote to leisure activities. However, this development has a major downside. It affects people's health, because not all people use the extra time to lead active lives. Consequently, obesity has increased among all ages, resulting in serious health problems like heart disease.*
>
> *Electronic devices such as tablets and mobile phones have made working and studying easier. Business people, for example, can communicate with people around the world using the internet. Moreover, as students can access libraries using their tablets or increasingly their mobile phones, they can now study anywhere, for example at home or in cafés. However, this has brought about some disadvantages such as increased inactivity and reduced socialization, which affect the individual and society.*

> *Another positive development is that robots in factories have increased productivity. In many industries, such as car manufacturing, and agriculture, most of the heavy work is now done by machines, which has meant that more goods can be produced at lower cost. Although these developments are beneficial, they have led to job losses, for example, in banking where many jobs are being replaced by automated processes.*
>
> *As we have seen, while machines have had a positive impact on our lives, there are some important drawbacks that cannot be ignored.*

Word count: 279 words

Comments

The introduction paraphrases the topic in the Writing Task on page 123 (keeping the word *machines* but expressing the rest in different words, including different words for *advantages* and *disadvantages*). The introduction clearly states that advantages and then disadvantages are going to be discussed in that order (each one in three paragraphs, or advantages and the disadvantages in separate paragraphs). There is clear paragraphing and paragraphs are all connected to the introduction using clear topic sentences (the first sentence in each body paragraph), as is the conclusion which refers back to the introduction and the topic in the Writing Task.

The text contains a wide range of vocabulary including collocations, e.g. *give … freedom, devote time to, lead … lives*. The ideas are signalled clearly using linking devices, e.g. *because, consequently, resulting in, another, although*, and there are reasons and examples in each paragraph, e.g. *have given people more freedom – more time for leisure activities, have made working and studying easier – communicate around the world and study anywhere; increased productivity – more goods produced*. Note also the use of complex sentences, e.g. *Consequently, …, resulting in …, Moreover, as … for example … .*

Version 2

> *Machines are increasingly doing many tasks, both in the home and the workplace, that were done by humans. This has brought many benefits. There is no denying that there are drawbacks.*
>
> *A major advantage is that domestic devices like dishwashers and washing machines, and now robotic vacuum cleaners have made people's lives more comfortable. These devices have given people more freedom. They allow them more time to devote to leisure activities and spend time with their families. However, this development has a major downside. It affects people's health. Not all people use the extra time to lead active lives. Consequently, obesity has increased among all ages, resulting in serious health problems like heart disease and diabetes.*
>
> *Electronic devices like tablets and mobile phones have made working and studying easier. People communicate with people around the world using the internet. And students can access libraries using their tablets or increasingly their mobile phones. They can study anywhere, at home, or in cafés. This has brought about some disadvantages such as more inactivity and less socialization. This affects the individual and society.*
>
> *Robots in factories have increased productivity. In many industries, most of the heavy work is now done by machines, which has meant that more goods can be produced at lower cost. These developments are beneficial, but they have led to job losses in banking where many jobs are being replaced by automated processes.*
>
> *While machines have had a positive impact on our lives, there are some important drawbacks that cannot be ignored.*

Word count: 252 words

Comments

The introduction paraphrases the topic in the Writing Task on page 123, and the answer is error-free. However, the sentences are generally not well connected. For example, in the introduction the connections could be signalled more using *but* to link the last two sentences, and adding a noun such as *development* after *this* in the second sentence. Throughout the answer, a few more phrases could be included to indicate examples (*For example, these devices have given …, People, for example, …*) and reasons (*It affects people's health, because not all people use the extra time to lead active lives*).

Moreover, the vocabulary could be more varied (*devices/appliances* and *people/business people*) and more examples could be given (*such as car manufacturing and agriculture*). Likewise, there could be more signalling of ideas (*Another positive development is that, as*).

Overall, the lack of examples, reasons and cohesion through proper linking of ideas affect the clarity of the answer.

PAGES 125–126
Speaking Part 2

Further Practice and Guidance (page 126)

Possible answer:

– There were many rules that I agreed with when I was at school, but the one I am going to talk about is *the banning of mobile phones in lessons*.
– The reason I agreed with this rule was *that students' phones were ringing and bleeping during lessons and this was very disruptive*.
– The introduction of this rule had a number of effects on life in the school. Firstly, *lessons were not interrupted by ringing or bleeping phones*. And secondly, *students were not distracted by reading and sending text messages* and also *the majority thought the rule was fair, because they could still use their phones in school, but only in break times*.
– In my opinion, this rule was a good thing, because *lessons are no longer interrupted, and students are not distracted by the use of mobile phones*. Another positive effect was *that concentration levels in lessons generally have improved as a result*.

PAGES 125–127
Speaking Part 3

Further Practice and Guidance (pages 126–127)

1

Rules in everyday life
a Example 2: *work regulations*
   Example 3: *rules of the law*
b Example 2: *inconvenient*
   Example 3: *pointless*
c Effect 2: *lack of progress*
   Effect 3: *disorder*

2

Possible answers:

Rules in everyday life

What rules are most common in everyday life?

I suppose there are rules in every aspect of life, but the most common examples I can think of would be school rules and regulations at work. Of course, there is also the law, and the rules of the law cover almost every area of life.

How do you think people feel about rules in everyday life?

I think that depends on both the person and the rule. In my own opinion, rules are necessary. For example, rules are essential at school – maybe teenagers don't like them, but the rules are there for their benefit. Other people might find rules inconvenient, like at work. For example, you might not be allowed to use a smartphone or take your lunch when you would like to. Another aspect about rules is that people sometimes break them – take the rules of the law about driving, for instance. Using a phone while driving, not wearing a seat belt, speeding – there are regulations about all of these things, but they are often ignored, in which case people might think these rules are pointless.

How would everyday life be different if there were no rules?

That's a difficult question, and again, I think it depends on which rules you are talking about. If there were no rules at school, there would be chaos. Students would be late, never do their homework and be disruptive in class. Or if there were no regulations at work, nobody would meet any deadlines and there wouldn't be any progress or productivity. If there were no laws in everyday life, I think society would descend into disorder so, overall I think that rules are essential – even if we don't like them at times.

Listening scripts

Test 1 Section 1

Questions 1–6

Maxine Mr Bird?

Mr Bird Yes.

Maxine I'm Maxine Johnson, the garden designer you rang.

Mr Bird Thank you for coming and for being so punctual, dead on 2pm.

Maxine I always try to arrive on time. Sometimes it doesn't happen, though. Have you just moved to the area?

Mr Bird Yes, we came here just three weeks ago. It's a nice area.

Maxine It's really quiet and there are lots of trees. Is the garden you want me to design for you at the back?

Mr Bird Yes, that's the garden that needs tidying up. I've taken out all the rubbish and cut the grass back, but it needs some design to liven it up.

Maxine I'm sure that can be easily done.

Mr Bird If you come through, you can see for yourself. We can go through the gate here at the side of the house ... And here it is.

Maxine It's quite large, in fact, bigger than I thought it would be.

Mr Bird Yes, it's 25 metres long. So we've got plenty of room to play with.

Maxine Have you got any thoughts about what you'd like?

Mr Bird Oh, yes. We'd like a wooden patio built here from the house into the garden with enough room for a round table, chairs and a barbecue and then a lawn.

Maxine And what size would you like to have?

Mr Bird Mmm ... say ... 16 square metres.

Maxine Anything else?

Mr Bird Mmm. A small pond, but I don't want any fish ... and a water fountain in the middle with some lights would be nice.

Maxine And again, the size of the pond?

Mr Bird About two metres across.

Maxine That sounds nice – you seem to have thought it all through. What I can do is put the information you give me into my tablet as we speak, and then we can look at a rough design when we've finished.

Mr Bird Oh, wow. That sounds very fancy.

Maxine It saves a lot of time and can give us a basic idea of costs. And we can then finalize everything later.

Mr Bird Brilliant.

Maxine So, we've got the patio, the pond and the fountain.

Mr Bird Right. And then just beyond the pond we'd like to have a fence, say two metres high, with climbing flowers and then a door in the middle leading into a vegetable garden for growing herbs and potatoes, cabbage and beans, things like that.

Maxine Hmm.

Questions 7–10

Maxine Does all this look OK?

Mr Bird Yes. That looks great. It's amazing what technology can do.

Maxine I can email this to you so you can think about it. When you decide you want to go ahead, we can finalize it and work out the cost.

Mr Bird Great.

Maxine Can I take your email address?

Mr Bird Hmm ... it's nick@neworchard.com – no spaces.

Maxine Is that n-i-c-k then @ and o-r-c-h-a-r-d dot com?

Mr Bird No, it's *new* orchard.com. Hmm ... can I just ask you when you can start and how long it'll take?

Maxine It's Wednesday today. Hmm ... I can start next Monday, that's the 11th.

Mr Bird OK, the 11th July. And how long will it take?

Maxine Hmm. It's a fairly big job and with two workers, it's going to take ten working days.

Mr Bird That sounds reasonable. I'll talk this over with my wife and then get back to you tomorrow first thing.

Maxine That sounds fine. If you want to go ahead with everything, can you decide if the plan works for you?

Mr Bird Yes, sure. I'll give you my work mobile number as that's the one that's best to contact me on.

Maxine OK, fire away.

Mr Bird It's 07811 499466.

Maxine ... 499466.

Mr Bird Yes. And can you give me a rough estimate of the cost for now?

Maxine With the materials, I'd say about ...

Test 1 Section 2

Questions 11–14

Arnold I know there's an action-packed weekend in store for those of you heading to the capital, so I'm going to hand you over to Martina, who will tell you what you can expect to find when you get here ...

Martina Thank you, Arnold. Well, yes, this weekend seems to have a greater number of events going on than usual, and so I expect that large crowds will be using the transport system. The main shopping street in the city centre, Argent Street, is going to be closed to all traffic including buses from 1am until 10pm on Saturday. This is because there will be an International Food Festival, the Food of Life Festival, which will be held on the street with stalls and street entertainment for all the family.

The closure of Argent Street will, unfortunately, affect all the surrounding streets, and so it's best to avoid the city by car on Saturday. There will be extra buses, but remember some of them will be diverted to avoid the festival. But at most of the central bus stops, there'll be guides who'll be in yellow jackets, who can help visitors find their way around. The best way of getting to the Food Festival is probably by the river bus, which stops near the festival. The river buses will be increased in frequency to every ten minutes from twice an hour. Also the train service will be running extra trains for the day.

One important piece of information that I need to point out to you is that the profits from the Food Festival will go to various charities helping young people in this country and around the world.

Questions 15–20

In the Food of Life Festival, there won't just be food on display. There'll also be a play area for children, folk music with bands, solo singers and artefacts from different countries. For example, in the park behind the train station, there'll be the Asian sector with food stalls from China, Japan and Korea as well as Indonesia and the Philippines, and a concert will be held at 2pm for folk music. And beside the station is a Help Point if people lose their friends or children during the day.

Just a few hundred yards south of the Help Point on the same side of the road and opposite the European Food Sector is something which is well worth visiting. There'll be a display of sculptures made from chocolate not just by famous chocolate manufacturers but also by artists, with a prize-giving at 5pm. You cannot miss it as it's right next to the old cinema, which is also an exciting place to visit. It'll be open for visits from 10am till 5pm with guided tours every 20 minutes. The cinema is located just opposite the Latin American food display, which will also have music and dancing classes. Then further south along the street will be a craft fair in Cannery Hall, which is on the corner of Argent Street and Churchill Avenue.

A further attraction is that all of the permanent shops will be offering a minimum discount of 10% and you can also claim a 20% discount at all restaurants and cafés between 12 noon and 5pm and all children up to the age of ten eat for free.

And that's not all, after 5pm all the produce on the stalls in the Food Festival will be offered at a 25% discount, so it is a worthwhile day out for the whole family. At 9pm just before the festival finishes, there will be a 15-minute firework display and street music.

Test 1 Section 3

Questions 21–23

Cheng What are you doing your essay on, Antonia?

Antonia I was originally going to do a comparison between French and Chinese cinema, but it's quite a big topic.

Cheng Yeah, it is.

Antonia So I've decided to restrict it to one decade, the 1970s. And I've actually got my first draft.

Cheng How much have you written?

Antonia At the moment, it's about 7,000 words, so that's around 2,000 words too long. I didn't intend to write so much!

Cheng Wow. You've written loads! How did you manage to get that amount done?

Antonia I suppose I've just been thinking of it as two essays really to help me get through it and I've been using the checklist we got in the tutorial from Dr Nakamura, not the checklist you and I created ourselves.

Cheng And are you happy with your draft?

Antonia Mmm ... I'm fairly happy with it. I usually think I can't write very much and then when I get down to it, it's the opposite.

Cheng Mhmm.

Antonia But I also need to go through it and check for errors in typing and also check it from the organizational point of view, which is going to be time-consuming. So I'll probably leave the checking to the end, as I'm likely to add mistakes when I start cutting and redrafting.

Questions 24–30

Antonia What about you, Cheng? How much have you written?

Cheng About 5,000 words, but it's just disjointed notes really, and the main issue is that there's no structure. But apart from the structure being a problem, I really have difficulty focusing. I usually have lots of ideas, but connecting them is a different matter.

Antonia Er ... What do you think the reason is?

Cheng Probably not having a specific title. I just can't make up my mind about what to focus on. I write notes and can write quite a lot and talk loads about the subject I've chosen, but ...

Antonia What's the general topic of your essay?

Cheng Chinese photography.

Antonia Well, why not restrict yourself to one or two perspectives like technological or cultural, or to developments in a particular period, say pre-1990s and write about developments in the pre-Digital Age?

Cheng That's an idea. I can see that now – I think you've solved my problem. I'd better write this down. I wish we'd talked before. I wouldn't have wasted so much time.

Antonia I hope it works.

Cheng Any tips about introductions, another of my problems? I can never get the beginning right.

Antonia The main reason's not knowing what the stages of the introduction are. They're quite specific. Look at Student Support pages on the university website and you'll find the answer there. Search for 'stages in writing introductions and conclusions'.

Cheng Another problem solved!

Antonia Anything else?

Cheng Hmm ... I think redrafting when I get round to it. I'm not good at it at all. In fact, I hate looking at it when it's finished.

Antonia I know what you mean. Oh, we all suffer from that. I'm not sure what makes us feel like that. Maybe, it's just fear of going back to the beginning again.

Cheng You're probably right. And I don't think there is any solution for that, bar getting down to it.

Antonia Well, you could try writing a summary of your essay at the end and then see if the essay matches the summary.

Cheng Oh, that's a good strategy. Mmm. But why leave us to do this all without specific guidance? I find it quite difficult working on my own like this. I'm not used to it.

Antonia It's not that easy for most students. Essays or any project like this are to encourage and train students in independent learning.

Cheng It's independent all right. What's the deadline again?

Antonia Mmm ... It's the 17th of March, so we have another three weeks.

Cheng Oh, that's fine. I thought it was the end of the first week in March. That would've made it difficult.

Antonia I'd say aim to have a draft ...

Test 1 Section 4

Questions 31–40

Good morning to you all and thank you for coming today. My name's Dr John Morton. For those of you who don't know me, I'm a research fellow in the Geography Department and my speciality is change in agricultural patterns around the world, historically and in modern times. Today's talk is called *Agriculture – re-greening the deserts of the world*. The lecture's being recorded, so you can review it again on the university website within 48 hours.

First of all, in the distant past, between 8,000 and 5,500 years ago, the Sahara, for example, was green and fertile. The world temperature was roughly the same as today's, but with little weather that was wild ... such as hurricanes. At this time, areas of the world in the African, Asian and American continents, which are now covered by desert, had more water than they do now. If we look at this slide of an artist's impression of the Sahara of that time, as you can see, the Sahara was not always so dry: there were rivers, swamps and lakes, some of them very large.

Lake Chad, for example, which today is only several hundred square kilometres, was once a huge inland sea. In total, it covered an area equivalent to France, Germany, Spain and the UK together. At various periods, the lake broke its banks and flowed through Nigeria into the Atlantic or the Nile in the east. Another interesting fact, as you'll see from another artist's impression of the weather map on this slide, was that the whole of North Africa was subject to a monsoon system like that in Asia today, resulting in vast rivers that flowed for thousands of kilometres.

In Algeria, underground rivers have been found that flowed into the Mediterranean, and in southern Libya crocodile, elephant, hippo and antelope bones have been discovered. And of interest to me as an agriculturist, there is also evidence of some of the earliest fields growing grain.

If we fast-forward to the modern world, are such changes likely to happen again? While what brings about these changes is complex and open to furious debate, there is no doubt that changes can and will happen and we have to be ready for them. But this is not just about the flooding, severe winter weather, storms, droughts and so on, that have happened in recent years, but about how it'll affect our livelihoods.

As regards challenges for humanity, the first thing that we have to think about generally is food security. If, as seems to be happening, Europe continues to warm up, then cereal crops like wheat and barley and fruit crops that we have depended on may not be suitable for cultivation. The UK, for example, might have to turn to producing grapes and olives and other crops suitable for hotter climates. This situation may be further compounded by countries in Southern Europe, which may find their ability to produce agricultural goods severely curtailed. The overall impact will be an increase in food prices in Europe, but the impact on poorer countries will be greater.

Yet there is hope. With the shift in weather patterns around the world, there's strong evidence that vegetation is increasing in certain areas that were once desert. The Sahel, for example, has seen increased vegetation cover, and so there is a chance that water might return to vast areas like the Sahara and the other great deserts of the world.

So the re-greening of the ...

Test 2 Section 1

Questions 1–6

Ricky Hello, Firstlife Insurance. My name's Ricky. Can I help you?

Daniella Yes, I hope so. I'm looking to get some more information about health insurance.

Ricky OK. And can you give me your full name?

Daniella Daniella Forbes.

Ricky ... Forbes. I can help you, of course, but you do know all our information is on the website.

Daniella Oh yes, I know. I got your details from a health insurance comparison website, but when I went on it the website kept freezing, so I took your number and thought I'd ring you.

Ricky Oh, I'm sorry about that. So what would you like to know?

Daniella Mmm, could you tell me how much it costs to cover the whole family for a year?

Ricky If I can take a few details, I can type them in and then we'll get a figure. How many people are we talking about?

Daniella Two adults and two children.

Ricky OK, and could you tell me the ages of your children?

Daniella A boy, Charles, 7 and a girl, Aimie, 9.

Ricky And could you give me your ages?

Daniella My husband, John, is 31 and I'm 33.

Ricky ... 31 and 33. Mmm, and your occupations?

Daniella We're both in education. My husband's a primary school teacher and I'm a college lecturer.

Ricky Fine. And ... mmm ... in the past, have any of you had any major illnesses, like ...?

Daniella Actually, none at all.

Ricky And does that include your children?

Daniella Oh, yes.

Ricky That's good. And do you or your husband smoke?

Daniella No.

Ricky And have you had health insurance before?

Daniella No.

Ricky OK. And are you looking for a plan that gives comprehensive cover?

Daniella Yes, we want cover for the dentist, the optician, and the doctor and hospital stays.

Ricky Fine. Let's see. What about alternative therapies?

Daniella Like what?

Ricky Acupuncture, physiotherapy?

Daniella Mmm ... are they covered in the comprehensive plan?

Ricky Yes ... you do know that you can also select individual plans.

Daniella Yes, mmm, but we want full cover for the whole family.

Ricky OK. I'll just put in these details and see what the computer comes up with.

Questions 7–10

Daniella And the cost?

Ricky For comprehensive cover for the whole family it's showing £73.59 per month.

Daniella For the four of us for everything?

Ricky Yes.

Daniella That's really reasonable. If we go on to the website again, will all the information still be there?

Ricky Oh yes, I can give you a reference number. Have you got a pen?

Daniella Just hold on ... OK. I'm ready.

Ricky It's PB663885FJ.

Daniella Did you say SG?

Ricky No, FJ.

Daniella OK. Got it.

Ricky Oh, and I should mention the discount. If you take out the insurance, you get the first two months for free.

Daniella That's worth having.

Ricky Yes. It helps quite a lot. And another thing you might be interested in is that if you recommend friends and they take out the insurance, you get £50 worth of book vouchers.

Daniella Oh, great. I have several friends who may be interested.

Ricky You can pay online for the year in advance or you can set up a payment to be taken out of your bank each month.

Daniella OK.

Ricky I can set things up for you and you can think about it and complete everything online.

Test 2 Section 2

Questions 11–17

Caroline Now we're going over to David, who's going to talk briefly about what visitors to St John's and the surrounding area can expect to see.

David Thank you, Caroline. The town is well known for its pretty buildings in local stone along with an internationally famous golf course and its castle ruins on the edge of the town, but if you prefer shopping or eating instead of sightseeing, you won't be disappointed as the town has plenty to offer for a wide range of tastes. You won't find amusement arcades here, nor will you find any fast-food restaurants, but we have restaurants specializing in local dishes using local products as well as a wide range of independent coffee shops and tea shops. In fact, the town is famous for not having any chain cafés, restaurants or shops, which is why it attracts lots of visitors especially in the summer. And we also have several local bookshops, which are a focal point for reading groups, and a literary festival which is held once a year.

But you don't have to go far if it's sand and sea and all the entertainment that goes with them that you're looking for. There are four local beaches that cater for all tastes. There are two beaches that are a 15-minute bus ride away, both to the south-east of the town and both facing south, so they catch the sun all day. Black Rock is probably the quieter of the two as it's small. The buses run there once an hour, but there are no shops or refreshment facilities around and parking is not easy. There's no car park, so visitors have to leave their vehicles along the roads approaching the beach.

Sandy Beach is very different. It has easy access to the town and you can walk there along a promenade and get to the beach easily. And if you have things to carry, there is a huge car park with lots of space, as well as a very frequent bus service every five minutes. This is one of the reasons why Sandy Beach is very suitable for families. It's also good for swimmers as the area near the shore is very shallow.

There are two other small beaches that are further along the coast to the west of Black Rock Beach. Port Tray is the first. It's very popular with surfers especially at weekends as it has huge waves, so it's not very suitable for swimmers. As the young crowd seem to like this place, it can be a bit noisy in the evenings and weekends. This beach is not really for families with children or older people.

The fourth beach is Little Cove, an area of outstanding natural beauty. It is easily accessible on foot, but you have to walk down a fairly steep cliff path to get to the beach. Once you're there, there's nothing but a beautiful curved beach with crystal clear water and more often than not very few people. It's something that shouldn't be missed.

Questions 18–20

But there are also plenty of activities for individual tourists and families in the surrounding countryside, if you don't fancy shopping or the beach. There are villages with old houses to visit and farms where you can pick your own fruit ... and some farms also have activities for children, like helping with the animals. And, of course, there are cliff top walks along the coast and walks in the woodlands, which are popular for picnics, and there are also river activities like canoeing and swimming. If you want more information about these and other facilities in the area, contact the local Tourist Centre.

Test 2 Section 3

Questions 21–27

Tutor We've got a couple of minutes left. So Tanya and Carlo, have you got any questions about your seminars next week and the week after?

Tanya Is it OK if I go first?

Carlo Yeah, no problem. There are just a few things I'd like to check.

Tutor Your seminar's going to be on ...?

Tanya At first, I was going to do it on sugar in the future, but then decided on a different commodity, corn.

Carlo I thought you were going to do it on ... metals and oil.

Tanya No, nothing like that ... I'm looking at corn and ... mmm ... the implications for several countries of a rise in prices because of ... population growth.

Carlo That sounds really interesting.

Tutor So, what do you want to ask about?

Tanya I wanted to ask about the overall organization of the slides to see if you think it's OK. I've got some slides here on my tablet, but I haven't finalized them yet.

Tutor OK. Let's have a look.

Tanya For example, ... the table on this slide gives the ranking of the top corn exporters I'm using as examples, along with some statistics and comments. You can see that the United States is first with export volumes of 513,834 million tonnes, and it has 36% of world corn production. And then in about a decade from now it is expected that overall production will increase by 50%.

Tutor Mhmm.

Tanya ... and the UK is ranked third with exports of 114 million tonnes. At the moment, the EU overall is responsible for 3% of world production, but that should increase in the future. And Chile comes fifth with only six million tonnes, but Latin America overall has enormous untapped potential as it has about 40% of the world's uncultivated cropland.

Tutor Fascinating.

Tanya So in future, a lot of grain in the world may come from Latin America. But, if that potential is not realized with rising population increases and occasional crop failures as a result of natural disasters, feeding the whole world could be a problem in the future.

Tutor It sounds as if your talk will be very thought-provoking, but I'd try and get the slides down to about 15, excluding the title page.

Tanya Mmm. All right. I'll aim for 16 then.

Tutor Is there anything else?

Questions 28–30

Tanya But how can I stop myself reading from a script? I'll be so nervous if I don't have one to read from. I don't mind answering questions at the end, but I get really nervous when speaking in front of people.

Tutor Carlo. What about you?

Carlo I used to be much the same, but I've been practising with friends. I talk about the PowerPoints and I've managed to keep it to 20 minutes. To help make myself focus, I've put the slides on a timer, so I have only two minutes per slide. This has really made me concentrate.

Tanya Oh, that's a neat idea.

Carlo I can show you how to do it and practise with you, if you want.

Tanya Would you?

Tutor Problem seems to have been solved then. Carlo, is there anything you want to talk about for your presentation?

Carlo I think I'm OK about everything, but ... maybe one thing ... mmm ... what about animation? Is it OK to use special features like that?

Tutor By all means, yes. But be careful.

Test 2 Section 4

Questions 31–40

Today, I'm going to give some feedback on our project on the latest developments in wearable technology, which is exciting everyone in the Fashion Department at the moment. Wearable technology is having a huge impact on the fashion world from tech glasses to smart fabrics that incorporate monitors and respond to light and human activity. Soon you'll be able to charge your mobile phone from electricity generated by solar panels in your clothes.

My colleagues and I have been working on a Design Project, which is partly funded by a government grant specifically in order to help establish links between the Fashion Department and young technology companies outside the university.

First of all, I'd like to point out there are different teams that we're working with inside the university, not just those in the Technology Institute, but also Sports, Science and Health. The products that we're working on may be design-led, but we would not be able to function without the two local tech companies we're involved with. The main benefit of this cooperation is that in the end, it has led to the products that we're working on appealing much more to the commercial world, which in turn has raised the department's profile considerably. A direct consequence of this enhanced reputation is that we've received increased research funding from other outside agencies not just the government, but sponsorships from fashion and sports companies.

Fashion design plays a central role in all wearable tech products if they are to appeal to a wider market. Early examples of products we made were clumsy and not very attractive and awkward to wear, as it was difficult to put the technology and garments such as shirts or vests together ... but the latest versions are very promising indeed.

We've just started looking at fashion items that monitor sports people's activities. They're already in common use, but we're concentrating on additional accessories such as bracelets that will appeal to the general public because of their design, not just their function. We may find that bracelets will one day be incorporated into socks to monitor runners' performance and ability and reduce injury. This is not a mile away from health monitors looking at the heart, breathing and general performance after an operation.

However, there's no doubt that there are challenges. The general public may not be ready for more technology *and technology* in their clothes as well, and the extra cost may put a lot of people off, so what we need to do above everything else is somehow come up with something that works well, is attractive to the public and inexpensive. As I just mentioned, we also have to bear in mind that people may be technology-weary, so we have to be careful about introducing the products at the right time, and ... mmm ... catching the eye of the public through careful advertising.

One downside of all these developments is people being overly obsessed with the data, and more stressed. Like their mobile phones, people may not be able to go out without their wearable tech accessories. But if they are used sensibly, then this won't happen.

What's more, the care of the garments might put people off. We have to ensure that neither the fabrics, nor the technology are destroyed through cleaning. We're looking at using special coatings that prevent the technology from being destroyed when washed again and again. We're being helped in this regard by the fact that technology is becoming smaller and easier to work with.

And the first item to go into production ...

Test 3 Section 1

Questions 1–6

Marina Hi, I understand you do short-term storage for students.

Man Yes, we do.

Marina Oh, great!

Man So, how can I help you?

Marina Well, it's nearly the end of term and I'm going back home for the summer, so I need to move all my belongings out of my house and put them somewhere safe.

Man Yes, well we can certainly arrange that for you. Can I start by asking you a few general questions before I take your personal details?

Marina Yeah, sure. That's OK.

Man First of all, how much stuff do you want to store?

Marina Mmm, I'm not sure. It's ...

Man OK, is it just books?

Marina Well ... mmm ... it's books ... about 60, I guess ... clothes from the wardrobe, winter clothes, some cooking utensils, like a few pots and pans, and ... mmm ... some furniture.

Man OK, and what kind of furniture?

Marina Mmm, there's a sofa, two chairs and a desk. The rest of the furniture belongs to my landlord.

Man Can you tell me, are there any fragile items at all?

Marina No, I'm taking anything breakable home with me.

Man We do offer a specialist wrapping and packing service for fragile items.

Marina Mmm, it's OK. I don't think I'll need that, thank you.

Man Fine, well, we could probably fit all your stuff into about 15 boxes, which with the furniture should fit into one of our secure storage units.

Marina And how much will that cost?

Man It sounds as if you only need a small storage unit, so that would be £15 a week. And there's an additional charge of £1 per box, but they'll be delivered to you free.

Marina Fine. That sounds reasonable. Just one thing though – I'm worried about boxes being lost.

Man There's no need to worry. When you've filled the boxes, they're all put together and wrapped in plastic and put with the furniture in the storage unit. And then you get a bar code with a reference number.

Marina Ah, OK. That sounds fine.

Man So, when would you like us to pick the stuff up?

Marina Mmm, today's Monday ... is Thursday of next week OK? That's June 24th.

Man Morning or afternoon?

Marina Morning, if possible.

Man That's fine, and we'll need a date to bring your things back.

Marina Let me think ... ideally, the 27th of August.

Questions 7–10

Man OK, I need to take some personal details. Your name is?

Marina Marina.

Man M-A-R-I-N-A, and your surname?

Marina Beech, as in the tree not the seaside.

Man So that's B-double E-C-H.

Marina That's it.

Man And what's the collection address?

Marina 37, Turnpike Road, Vale, and the postcode is NW3 0SR.

Man Mmm ... postcode NW3 0SR.

Marina So, you'll collect the filled boxes and the furniture a week on Thursday then?

Man Yes.

Marina Great, and what about getting the boxes so I can get started on the packing?

Man Let me see ... mmm ... one of our drivers'll be in your area tomorrow afternoon, that's June the 14th, so he can let you have the boxes then.

Marina Great, any other details you need?

Man I think that's about it. You can check the provisional booking on our website, and if it's OK with you, make the payment online and we'll take it from there.

Marina I'll do that this afternoon. Do I need a reference number?

Man Yes, I'll give you that now. Have you got a pen?

Marina Yeah, go ahead.

Man The booking reference is 726394, I for indigo, K for kilo.

Marina So that's 726394IK.

Man Yes, and that's all organized then. Any other queries?

Marina No, that's great. Thanks for all your help.

Man You're very welcome ...

Test 3 Section 2

Questions 11–16

Interviewer In the studio today, we have Diana Monroe, who has come to talk to us about a very successful local venture, The Hope Centre. Diana, can you tell us about how the new centre came about?

Diana Yes, of course. Good morning and thank you for having me here. The centre opened in March and even though we're only in September, it actually seems like it's been open for much longer! So, where shall I start? Well, we were initially planning just to renovate the centre by doing some painting inside and out, but we were successful in a bid for funding, which we really didn't expect to win. So, in the end, we decided to go for a much more extensive renovation. After the centre committee had agreed on the extent of the renovation at their Annual General Meeting, we hired an architect to design a new centre using the old building as a core.

Interviewer What changes did you make?

Diana Well, we did five things. First of all, we used to have our meetings in a local café, because we didn't have a room that we could invite people to. But now we've got a very modern room for training that we can also use for meetings. Another thing is that we extended one of the rooms to make a large hall. At first, we had planned to extend it only a little, but we built a hall which is big enough for indoor sports such as indoor football and basketball for young people and adults.

The third thing is that we added a new reception area. We used to have only a small windowless office, but we knocked down one of the internal walls, made an open-plan office and added a reception with comfortable seating. Some people had initially wanted to have vending machines selling food and drinks in the reception, but we decided to open a small café instead.

Mmm, while the construction was going on, we changed our minds about the use of one of the rooms. We had intended to have one large room with computers, but we decided to have an information centre where people of all ages could come for advice. The information centre has computers, books, leaflets, a phone and comfortable chairs. We added several small rooms for one-to-one advice sessions and a larger room.

Questions 17–20

Interviewer Are a lot of people using the centre?

Diana Oh yes, a lot more than before. Young people especially didn't use to come to the centre as it was old-fashioned. But now we've got a good mix of local people of all ages. I think that is due to the new staff. And previously, we only had a receptionist, a committee and volunteers, but we appointed three new staff members. We made Akbar Iqbal the Youth Worker. He is responsible for all activities and events for young people. And he's very successful already – the under-15 football team won a cup recently.

Our Centre Manager is Maria Tuff. We were thinking of just giving this duty to one of the committee members, but in the end we advertised for a post and Maria started six months ago. She used to work for a national charity, so her experience is very useful. Her main responsibility is the smooth running of the centre.

And the other permanent post is a Volunteer Coordinator, Martin Webb. He brought a lot of expertise from his previous job, where he was helping to get young people into apprenticeships. He organizes a team of ten volunteers of all ages helping with the wide range of activities at the centre.

Test 3 Section 3

Questions 21–24

Mark Hi, Erica, I haven't seen you for ages. How are things going?

Erica Hi, Mark. Fine, thanks, but I've been really busy with my work placement.

Mark Of course, I forgot you were doing one too. Where is it you're doing it?

Erica The Aztec Commercial bank in the city. It's a great company to work for ... I'm learning a lot and enjoying it too.

Mark That's good to hear. My placement is a bit dull, to be honest. What makes yours so good?

Erica I suppose it's all down to their company working practices. They really look after their workers. The policy document of the bank describes them as an invaluable asset. And quite rightly. They recognize that the success of the business depends on the people that they have working for them. In addition, they say they're dedicated to providing a structured working environment.

Mark And what does that mean exactly?

Erica Well, as far as I understand it, it means that employees are encouraged to take an active and regular role in the day-to-day running of the company. The people I work with are very motivated.

Mark It sounds as if the bank's working practices are very effective. That's why your placement is proving to be enjoyable and rewarding.

Erica It certainly is, and it's good to see the results too. Over the last couple of months, I've been able to see how the working practices that we've been talking about really do work and result in real benefits for the customers and clients of the bank. But enough about me. How's your placement going?

Mark Not as well as yours, unfortunately, ...

Questions 25–30

Mark So, tell me more about what makes the working practices of the Aztec bank a success.

Erica OK, to start off with, generally there's an open door policy, so staff can talk to senior staff whenever they like.

Mark That sounds good.

Erica It is, and we also get regular internal emails, so everyone knows about any updates to systems and procedures in the bank. We have to confirm that we've understood by sending a return email. Then management knows that everyone understands what is going on.

Mark That's a good idea.

Erica Also, we have weekly team meetings, which are a chance to share information and ideas. They're a great opportunity to give and get feedback. They're quite informal, so it's not at all daunting to say what you think.

Mark Mhmm.

Erica Then, there are also monthly motivational meetings, in which your personal involvement in all aspects of the business is encouraged. I must admit it does work. I feel very involved and loyal to the bank.

Mark So, are employees assessed in any way?

Erica Yes, every three months an informal interview with staff is arranged with line managers, and, mmm they talk about progress so far and your objectives for the future. I've just had one, and they focus on enhancing your personal development, and encourage you to look for opportunities to progress within the company.

Mark I know they have a lot of branches, so you could even go abroad.

Erica Yes, it's possible, but I'm quite happy here. In fact, this branch is a great place to work. It's the kind of job I can see myself having when I finish my course. And another plus is that at the end of every financial year there's a bonus scheme, which means that the top achievers get a cash payment, and five extra days' holiday in the following year.

Mark That's a really good incentive, extra time off and money, the ideal combination.

Erica It certainly is. The bank also looks after its employees on a more long-term basis too. And biannually, they've got an official appraisal system, which is a more in-depth look at an individual's achievements and goals.

Mark Well, it all sounds great. I'm tempted to ask you to get me an application form!

Test 3 Section 4

Questions 31–40

Today I would like to talk to you about responsible tourism, starting with explaining exactly what it is, and moving on to discuss what we can do to be a responsible tourist ourselves.

To put it simply, responsible tourism is a different way of travelling. It's all about respecting and benefiting local people and the environment. So everyone involved – tourists, travel operators, governments and local communities – are asked to take responsibility for their actions, and also for the impact of their actions. It's all about creating better places for people to live in and to visit. In the past, the focus of responsible tourism was the Earth but in 2002, The Cape Town Declaration on Responsible Tourism in Destinations stated that the focus should also include local populations.

Responsible tourism should minimize the impact it has on the destination, and also have some benefits. To achieve this aim, local people should be involved in decisions, and ideally benefit from tourism. For example, in Tanzania the local Maasai people have a fair say in tourism, and also receive some money from the profits which the game reserves make. In a similar way, in parts of Indonesia, where diving is a popular tourist activity, tour operators have played an important role by developing different zones for diving and fishing. In this way, both tourists and local fishermen can benefit.

Another important aspect of responsible tourism is that it should aim to conserve the heritage of a country. Mass tourism tends to focus on an all-inclusive experience, where visitors often have no or very limited contact with the local people or environment, often never leaving the holiday complex they are delivered to.
In contrast, responsible tourism provides more enjoyable experiences for tourists, through connections with local people and their environment, so that visitors can learn about traditions, cultures and customs. In this way, visitors are able to have more 'real' travel experiences.

Moving on, how can we ourselves make sure that we are a responsible tourist? Overall, we need to make sure that we minimize the impact of our travel, and maximize the benefits of our visit for the local community and environment. So, how can we do this? Well, there are some basic guidelines to follow. Firstly, before we go, we can find out about the destination we're visiting, read travel articles and guidebooks, and it also helps to learn a bit of the language – the locals will appreciate this. Oh, and also, we need to think carefully about the clothes we pack. We're much more likely to get a warm welcome if we're dressed appropriately.

Secondly, when we're there, we need to be friendly and join in with local activities and festivals and try to shop locally, and if possible not buy imported goods. If a guide is needed, it's better to find a local one, as they'll have much more information. And we should also try to use public transport, as it's a great way to meet locals and reduce carbon emissions. On the other hand, what we mustn't do is buy products made from endangered species as it encourages illegal traders, and we should avoid taking stones or things from archaeological sites. If *everyone* did that, there would be none left!

Lastly, when we return home, it can make a huge difference if we give feedback to the tour operator, both on what we really enjoyed and on any improvements that could be made. It is also possible to actively participate in tourism blogs, to remind people to be responsible travellers and share experiences and any tips that we might have on how to be responsible.

Well, that's the end of my presentation. Thank you very much for listening.

Test 4 Section 1

Questions 1–5

Woman Good morning.

Man Good morning.

Woman Can I help you?

Man Yes, I hope so. My friends and I are in London for a few days, and, mmm, we'd like to see a few of the sights.

Woman Well, I can certainly help with that. Anything particular you'd like to see?

Man Mmm … not sure, really. There's so much to see, it's not easy choosing.

Woman Yes, London has a lot to offer … let's see … To start with, are you interested in historic London or more modern attractions?

Man Mostly the historic sights, but we don't want to miss out on what's new either.

Woman OK . There's Buckingham Palace, the Tower of London and Hampton Court Palace. They're all really popular royal attractions, and there's Windsor Castle too, but that's quite a way outside London.

Man Mmm … we've only got five days, so I think we'll have to stick to what's in London.

Woman Good plan. You want to enjoy yourselves, not end up rushing around everywhere. Now what about museums?

Man Yes, we'd like to visit a couple – nothing too serious, though!

Woman I think you'd like the Science Museum, and Madame Tussauds – the wax museum. Both have a lot of interactive exhibits, which makes them great fun.

Man Sounds good, what about art? Any good exhibitions on at the moment?

Woman Well, a visit to the Tate Modern's one not to miss.

Man I've heard it's got a very wide range of contemporary art from around the world. Mmm … what about more traditional stuff?

Woman If it's traditional you're after, I'd say the National Portrait Gallery would be a good choice, and they have up-to-date exhibitions as well.

Man Mmm … any other things to do?

Woman I'd say no visit to London is complete without a trip on The London Eye. It's a great chance to experience a view of the whole city from above, and to get some great photos.

Man Oh yes, my friend was telling me about it – that's a definite yes.

Woman You can even have a private capsule, if you book in advance. And if there are enough of you, it doesn't work out that expensive …

Questions 6–10

Man So, how about general tours? What would you suggest?

Woman Let me see … there's a river boat cruise, if you fancy a leisurely and relaxing day out. Or the open-top bus tours are very popular, if the weather's good. Or if you and your friends are fit, there are bicycle tours, which are very popular with younger tourists.

Man Which would you recommend?

Woman Well, I know the boat cruises have very knowledgeable and informative commentaries, but the bus tours have recorded talks in ten languages, and the good thing is you can hop on and off.

Man Mmm … and the bike tours?

Woman They're good because they're cheaper, and groups are usually small, but as I said you have to be fairly fit … but they do show you secret bits of London.

Man Well, there's certainly plenty to do. Can I take some of these leaflets?

Woman Help yourself, but if you've got a smartphone you might find it easier to download some apps.

Man Good point. Do most of the sights have one?

Woman Yes, they're really good these days, a lot are free. They have interactive features, and let you take photos and share them to your favourite social network.

Man That'll save me carrying loads of brochures and a camera then.

Woman It will, and most app tours are now in over 21 languages too.

Man That's good to know, but I'm going to stick to English. That way I'll carry on learning the language as well.

Woman Good idea. Now what about restaurants …

Test 4 Section 2

Questions 11–14

Anna So Jonathan, you're going to update the committee on how the plans for the open-air concert are going.

Jonathan Yes, Anna, thank you. And the short answer is very well, but I'd like to take some time to explain in detail how the organizing is progressing. As I'm sure you can imagine, there are lots of details to take into consideration.

To begin with … mmm … as we discussed previously, the idea behind the open-air concert is to arrange an event that would be enjoyable for the performers and the audience, and to do this as cheaply as possible. So what do we need? Well, the venue's obviously free and available as it's the school playing field. The next thing to consider is the weather. Of course, we're hoping for a sunny evening, but we need to be prepared for rain too. The local youth club have offered us the use of a waterproof canopy which needs a few minor repairs, and we also have the offer of a huge tent from a local hire company. It won't cost us anything – even without any advertising.

And the college in town have agreed the loan of a sound system. All we'll need to do is pay for the insurance of the equipment for the evening. Finally, food and drink for the event. The Catering Department of the college have offered their services free, and the school governors are likely to subsidize a barbecue, so it won't be expensive. We can easily organize a selection of soft drinks as well.

Questions 15–20

I think that's all we need for the actual event, but there are lots of other 'behind-the-scene' activities that need sorting out as well. The safety aspect is very important, and to avoid any accidents we'll need a clearly marked audience-free zone. The performers are asking for a three-hour set-up time, and we need to make sure there's good vehicle access for them too. This should be fine as the car park's right next to the playing field. I've done quite a lot of research and I've found out that one of the most important things we need close to the performance area is a suitable and safety-certificated power supply. I don't see this being too much of a problem as the changing rooms are at that end of the field. So we can use the electricity from there. I've done a full risk assessment, and there are limitations regarding the running of cables, but I'm confident we can meet the safety guidelines.

And, mmm, the last thing to think about is how we're going to let people know about the concert. The group that are performing give details of all their concerts on their website, as well as on their social media pages, but we need to advertise locally as well. I thought it would be a good idea if each class teacher organized a poster competition. We could put the posters that the children design up around the town, and offer free tickets for the concert to the best entries. I've also put an advert in next week's local paper, so overall I'd say we're pretty well prepared.

Now, does anyone have any …?

Test 4 Section 3

Questions 21–27

Brad Hi. I thought I was going to be late, but it looks as if you two have just arrived yourselves.

Sophie/Miyaki Hi, Brad.

Brad So … mmm … have either of you selected the article you want to critique or comment on? Miyaki?

Miyaki Mmm … yes, I've chosen something, but I'm still thinking what to do with it.

Brad Sophie?

Sophie Well … mmm … I've gone for this one on … restricting government funding of university courses to science, technology, engineering and mathematics.

Brad That sounds suitably controversial.

Sophie Yes, it is … a bit!

Miyaki What are you going to say about the article?

Sophie Well … mmm … my immediate reaction is that it's effectively nonsense!

Miyaki Ah? The article seems to have made you quite angry.

Sophie It has!

Miyaki You don't seem to be afraid of criticizing the article. I can't see how we can criticize people like professors and writers, etc.

Sophie Well, yes, we can. It's difficult if you think about who they are, but we're not writing about the writers, but the contents of the article.

Miyaki Mmm … OK, I'd not thought about that. Hmm … I suppose I'm thinking more of the people.

Sophie Yes. But we have to look at the sources that have been used in the article and what other people say as well. We have to remember that articles like this can have consequences for government attitudes to the funding of courses and hence affect people's lives and the economy and society at large.

Brad So what are you going to say in your comments about the article?

Sophie Well, I'm going to agree with some points, but I'll probably contradict the majority of what is said using recent research.

Miyaki Like what?

Sophie Well, I've got a rough table here on a piece of paper. So … for a start, the article says that more students will be equipped for a job in the modern world, but not everyone is suited to studying science, technology …

Miyaki You mean the STEM subjects?

Sophie Yeah, and … mmm … because all of us have different goals and personalities. And … secondly, the article says that certain subjects like art, drama and languages, etc are more hobbies than subjects and if people want to study them they should pay for them themselves. But these subjects are vital core subjects.

Miyaki Mmm.

Sophie The reason for this is that we need people, teachers to teach languages and businessmen and women who speak a wide range of languages. In the global world, it's not just sufficient to rely on one language such as English. Having different languages is good for business and good for the economy, so the government should make sure that universities offer as wide a range of subjects as possible.

Miyaki Yes, but …

Sophie Mmm … sorry, one minute. And thirdly, the writer even says extra money should be given to students and universities that train scientists and engineers. However, … enough money is pumped into these areas already. We do need engineers … er … but not at the expense of other investment in other subject areas.

Brad But don't you think then that it is justifiable for universities to concentrate on STEM subjects?

Sophie There is nothing wrong with concentrating on them, but not at the expense of the arts and social sciences.

Brad But don't you think that these are less important to society?

Sophie Definitely not!

Questions 28–30

Miyaki Mmm … I just want to check that I've got the organization of the critique correct.

Brad OK. What do you think it is?

Miyaki Mmm … well … am I right in thinking I should highlight the main points of the article and then create an outline using these points?

Brad Mmm.

Miyaki Then in writing I restate the main points with the main supporting evidence, but without inserting my own opinion.

Brad Mmm.

Miyaki Then, perhaps I should review everything to get rid of unnecessary or less important info. And then the tricky bit for me, which is to write a review of each point in my summary saying whether the author is accurate, or … mmm … clear.

Brad And you also need to comment on how effective the writer is, and mention any new contributions he or she has made to the field and also mention areas where the article might need improvement.

Miyaki Mmm … the last bit is the part I'm unsure about. I'm just going to play safe I think and agree with everything.

Brad You have to be careful with that. You also need to write about some strengths and weaknesses. For example, are the facts correct? You need to do some basic research on this. You'll be surprised what you find.

Miyaki And the conclusion …

Test 4 Section 4

Questions 31–40

Good morning, and welcome to the course review for the Diploma in Software Engineering, which is being led by myself and John. I'm going to look back over some of the important aspects of the diploma. One is the work experience element, which I hope now you'll all be able to see the benefits of. And another aspect I'm going to focus on is a compulsory module in the diploma, which I know you've all been exposed to, and which I think is essential for today's world and will be very relevant in the future; and that is entrepreneurship.

First of all, as regards work experience, all students on courses in the department have benefited from experience in software companies either *before* joining the diploma course or on day-release work attachments *during* the course. The reason that many such companies are clustered around the university is, as is probably apparent, that they've been set up mainly by past graduates of this course, and other courses in the department. Some of the seminars and lectures have also been given by past students from these companies, so they are inspiring role models and champions for the university. It's clear that we have a good track record of getting people into work!

And the advantage of gaining some kind of experience in the workplace? The work experience, which is at the core of this course, provides plenty of opportunities to put the theoretical aspect of the knowledge and skills learnt into practice. It's not enough just to learn the theories behind the software engineering; the practical side is vital. Employers don't just want qualifications. This doesn't mean that qualifications aren't important; they are. But practical experience in a workplace is important. In today's competitive global market, it is difficult and sometimes seemingly impossible to gain experience if you haven't got a job, but all students finishing the course are very well placed as far as the job market is concerned.

And the main advantage of the Entrepreneurship module? One current phenomenon that will benefit all young 'tech entrepreneurs' is current market trends, which will continue well into the future. While the future world is likely to be more dominated by global enterprises, business people and governments are also likely to emphasize the need for more small companies, such as flexible tech start-ups. These companies'll be able to react to changes in the market much more quickly than large companies, where decision-making can be slow and change difficult to enact. So the secret is to develop an enterprise that is dynamic and can respond fast to changing market trends.

The networking skills that you also focus on in the Entrepreneurship module in the diploma will also help everyone in their careers. Networking is a crucial skill that is needed out there in the real world of work. The course has provided ample opportunities for students to establish contacts and build up their own networks. In doing so, we also hope we've shown how systems within organizations work, and more importantly what aspects don't work. Everyone has also seen what it's like to put together a team of people to work on a project. If someone intends to 'go it alone', this will show what challenges might be faced. And, finally, networking provides a springboard for future developments and a chance to see if there are people out there that you could or would like to work with.

If 'going it alone' by setting up a business is the preferred option, it is important to keep in mind how the benefits of the entrepreneurship skills learnt on the course go beyond your own career. The skills that have been acquired on the course can open up economic potential and be a source of new jobs and growth. This can lead to economic independence and benefit the local economy, and incidentally the reputation of the university, especially this department.

In the World skills module, non-cognitive skills have been the main focus. These have included opportunity recognition, innovation, critical thinking, resilience, decision-making, teamwork and leadership. It is useful to reflect on these when working in the real world of work.

I'm now going to hand you over to my colleague John, who will talk to you about finance sourcing for setting up businesses on your own or even in conjunction with the university, including an exciting new pilot scheme, being launched this year, through which the university will part-fund new tech start-ups. So I'd like to take this opportunity to wish …

BRITISH COUNCIL

idp IELTS AUSTRALIA

CAMBRIDGE ENGLISH
Language Assessment
Part of the University of Cambridge

IELTS Listening and Reading Answer Sheet

Centre number:

Pencil must be used to complete this sheet.

Please write your **full name** in CAPITAL letters on the line below:

_____

Then write your six digit Candidate number in the boxes and shade the number in the grid on the right.

0 1 2 3 4 5 6 7 8 9
0 1 2 3 4 5 6 7 8 9
0 1 2 3 4 5 6 7 8 9
0 1 2 3 4 5 6 7 8 9
0 1 2 3 4 5 6 7 8 9
0 1 2 3 4 5 6 7 8 9

Test date (shade ONE box for the day, ONE box for the month and ONE box for the year):

Day: 01 02 03 04 05 06 07 08 09 10 11 12 13 14 15 16 17 18 19 20 21 22 23 24 25 26 27 28 29 30 31

Month: 01 02 03 04 05 06 07 08 09 10 11 12   **Year** (last 2 digits): 13 14 15 16 17 18 19 20 21

Listening Listening Listening	Marker use only	Listening Listening Listening	Marker use only
1	✓ 1 ✗	21	✓ 21 ✗
2	✓ 2 ✗	22	✓ 22 ✗
3	✓ 3 ✗	23	✓ 23 ✗
4	✓ 4 ✗	24	✓ 24 ✗
5	✓ 5 ✗	25	✓ 25 ✗
6	✓ 6 ✗	26	✓ 26 ✗
7	✓ 7 ✗	27	✓ 27 ✗
8	✓ 8 ✗	28	✓ 28 ✗
9	✓ 9 ✗	29	✓ 29 ✗
10	✓ 10 ✗	30	✓ 30 ✗
11	✓ 11 ✗	31	✓ 31 ✗
12	✓ 12 ✗	32	✓ 32 ✗
13	✓ 13 ✗	33	✓ 33 ✗
14	✓ 14 ✗	34	✓ 34 ✗
15	✓ 15 ✗	35	✓ 35 ✗
16	✓ 16 ✗	36	✓ 36 ✗
17	✓ 17 ✗	37	✓ 37 ✗
18	✓ 18 ✗	38	✓ 38 ✗
19	✓ 19 ✗	39	✓ 39 ✗
20	✓ 20 ✗	40	✓ 40 ✗

SAMPLE

Marker 2 Signature		Marker 1 Signature		Listening Total

IELTS L-R v1.0

denote Print Limited 0121 520 5100

DP787/394

Please write your **full name** in CAPITAL letters on the line below:

_____

Please write your Candidate number on the line below:

_____

Please write your three digit language code in the boxes and shade the numbers in the grid on the right.

0 1 2 3 4 5 6 7 8 9
0 1 2 3 4 5 6 7 8 9
0 1 2 3 4 5 6 7 8 9

Are you: Female? ▭   Male? ▭

Reading Reading Reading Reading Reading Reading

Module taken (shade one box):   Academic ▭   General Training ▭

#	Answer	Marker use only	#	Answer	Marker use only
1		✓ 1 ✗	21		✓ 21 ✗
2		✓ 2 ✗	22		✓ 22 ✗
3		✓ 3 ✗	23		✓ 23 ✗
4		✓ 4 ✗	24		✓ 24 ✗
5		✓ 5 ✗	25		✓ 25 ✗
6		✓ 6 ✗	26		✓ 26 ✗
7		✓ 7 ✗	27		✓ 27 ✗
8		✓ 8 ✗	28		✓ 28 ✗
9		✓ 9 ✗	29		✓ 29 ✗
10		✓ 10 ✗	30		✓ 30 ✗
11		✓ 11 ✗	31		✓ 31 ✗
12		✓ 12 ✗	32		✓ 32 ✗
13		✓ 13 ✗	33		✓ 33 ✗
14		✓ 14 ✗	34		✓ 34 ✗
15		✓ 15 ✗	35		✓ 35 ✗
16		✓ 16 ✗	36		✓ 36 ✗
17		✓ 17 ✗	37		✓ 37 ✗
18		✓ 18 ✗	38		✓ 38 ✗
19		✓ 19 ✗	39		✓ 39 ✗
20		✓ 20 ✗	40		✓ 40 ✗

SAMPLE

| Marker 2 Signature | | Marker 1 Signature | | Reading Total |

IELTS Results

After you have completed the IELTS test, you will receive a Test Report Form which details your score. For each module of the test (Listening, Reading, Writing and Speaking), you will receive a Band Score between 0 and 9. These individual module scores are then added together and averaged for an Overall Band Score reported as a whole band or a half band (e.g. 6.5). The table below gives a summary of the English of a candidate classified at each band level.

An IELTS Overall Band Score of 6.0 or 6.5 is usually required for entry to universities and colleges in Australia, New Zealand, Canada and the United Kingdom. However, some institutions may ask for a higher score.

BAND 9 – EXPERT USER
Has fully operational command of the language: appropriate, accurate and fluent with complete understanding.

BAND 8 – VERY GOOD USER
Has fully operational command of the language with only occasional unsystematic inaccuracies and inappropriacies. Misunderstandings may occur in unfamiliar situations. Handles complex detailed argumentation well.

BAND 7 – GOOD USER
Has operational command of the language, though with occasional inaccuracies, inappropriacies and misunderstandings in some situations. Generally handles complex language well and understands detailed reasoning.

BAND 6 – COMPETENT USER
Has generally effective command of the language despite some inaccuracies, inappropriacies and misunderstandings. Can use and understand fairly complex language, particularly in familiar situations.

BAND 5 – MODEST USER
Has partial command of the language, coping with overall meaning in most situations, though is likely to make many mistakes. Should be able to handle communication in own field.

BAND 4 – LIMITED USER
Basic competence is limited to familiar situations. Has frequent problems in understanding and expression. Is not able to use complex language.

BAND 3 – EXTREMELY LIMITED USER
Conveys and understands only general meaning in very familiar situations. Frequent breakdowns in communication occur.

BAND 2 – INTERMITTENT USER
No real communication is possible except for the most basic information using isolated words or short formulae in familiar situations and to meet immediate needs. Has great difficulty in understanding spoken and written English.

BAND 1 – NON USER
Essentially has no ability to use the language beyond possibly a few isolated words.

BAND 0 – DID NOT ATTEMPT THE TEST
No accessible information provided.

CD 1

TEST 1
01   Test instructions

Section 1
02   Instructions
03   Questions 1–6
04   Instructions
05   Questions 7–10
06   End-of-section instructions

Section 2
07   Instructions
08   Questions 11–14
09   Instructions
10   Questions 15–20
11   End-of-section instructions

Section 3
12   Instructions
13   Questions 21–23
14   Instructions
15   Questions 24–30
16   End-of-section instructions

Section 4
17   Instructions
18   Questions 31–40
19   End-of-test instructions

TEST 2
20   Test instructions

Section 1
21   Instructions
22   Questions 1–6
23   Instructions
24   Questions 7–10
25   End-of-section instructions

Section 2
26   Instructions
27   Questions 11–17
28   Instructions
29   Questions 18–20
30   End-of-section instructions

Section 3
31   Instructions
32   Questions 21–27
33   Instructions
34   Questions 28–30
35   End-of-section instructions

Section 4
36   Instructions
37   Questions 31–40
38   End-of-test instructions

CD 2

TEST 3
01   Test instructions

Section 1
02   Instructions
03   Questions 1–6
04   Instructions
05   Questions 7–10
06   End-of-section instructions

Section 2
07   Instructions
08   Questions 11–16
09   Instructions
10   Questions 17–20
11   End-of-section instructions

Section 3
12   Instructions
13   Questions 21–24
14   Instructions
15   Questions 25–30
16   End-of-section instructions

Section 4
17   Instructions
18   Questions 31–40
19   End-of-test instructions

TEST 4
20   Test instructions

Section 1
21   Instructions
22   Questions 1–5
23   Instructions
24   Questions 6–10
25   End-of-section instructions

Section 2
26   Instructions
27   Questions 11–14
28   Instructions
29   Questions 15–20
30   End-of-section instructions

Section 3
31   Instructions
32   Questions 21–27
33   Instructions
34   Questions 28–30
35   End-of-section instructions

Section 4
36   Instructions
37   Questions 31–40
38   End-of-test instructions
39   Title